WINNING ON THE INSIDE

Living Beyond Yesterday

The Road to Recovery
Over Bitterness and Unforgiveness

by
Brian Bohrer

Visit our website: www.pastorbrian.org

WINNING ON THE INSIDE — LIVING BEYOND YESTERDAY
"The Road to Recovery Over Bitterness and Unforgiveness"
ISBN 978-1-893019-50-8
Copyright ©1999, 2009 by Brian Bohrer
Second Printing 2009

Brian Bohrer Ministries
P. O. Box1577
Washington, Missouri 63090 USA
www.pastorbrian.org
Phone: (636) 239-5944

24/7 Faith Publications
P. O. Box 1577
Washington, Missouri 63090 USA

Editor: Marilyn Price
Cover Design: WildmanDesign

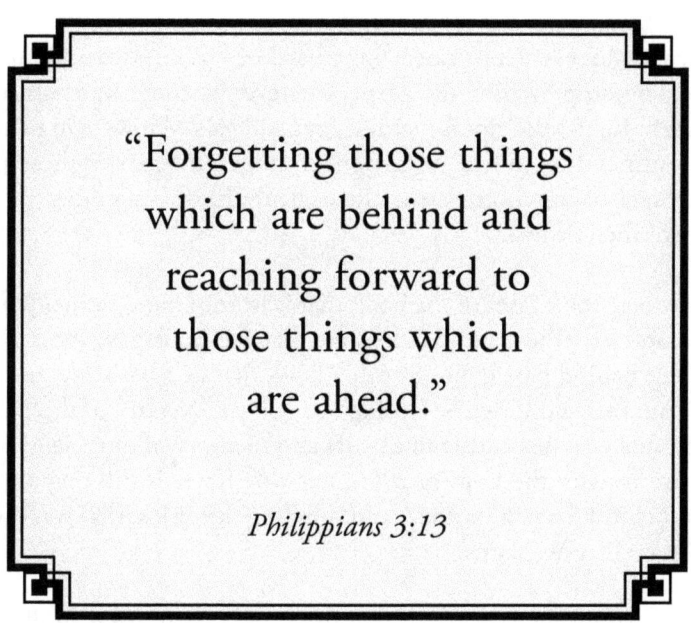

"Forgetting those things
which are behind and
reaching forward to
those things which
are ahead."

Philippians 3:13

In Memory of
Dr. Kenny Pete Williams

I met Kenny Pete Williams not long after he was released from prison in 1996. He was serving two life terms in the Mississippi Correctional Unit. During his time in prison, Kenny Pete was born again and was called to preach the gospel. He began studying the Word of God for six years through a correspondence course while in prison.

After serving seventeen years behind bars, he was released and immediately began preaching the gospel wherever he could find someone to listen. Kenny did not forget the guys and gals who were in prison. He continued to go back to prisons throughout America preaching the gospel of our Lord Jesus Christ. Truly he was a soldier in the army of the Lord.

Kenny Pete took cases of the book that is in your hand to many prisoners and gave them out. He told me that this book gave more hope to those behind bars than any other book that he gave away, and for this I am truly honored. So during our 10th anniversary of this book, I would like to dedicate it to the life and memory of our friend who went to be with the Lord in 2008. His wife Kayla is still praying for those behind the prison doors and fulfilling the vision that was given to Kenny Pete Williams.

If you would like to read the story of Kenny Pete Williams, go to **www.csfm.org** and you will find his testimony in his own words.

We will miss our friend and beloved in the Lord.

Preface

Have you ever heard these words: "Nobody knows what I am going through," or "I really screwed up my life," or "I ought to end it all because I have messed up other people's lives too"? These are some of the statements from the letters that we have received from people who learned to put their past behind them and to begin a new journey towards peace and hope.

No matter what has happened to you, no matter what you have done, you can begin again even at the bottom in life. You can rise up with the help of God and the help of His Word.

Life begins at the crossroads of change and most of all, at the place of forgiveness. There are two basic principles that this book goes over:

(1) Accepting forgiveness from God.

(2) Understanding His forgiveness will empower you to forgive yourself and others.

Forgiveness is something you accept and something you must give away!

I want to encourage you to begin and to finish the journey and I pray this book will help you discover that God loves you and that He has a great plan for your life.

Heartfelt thanks to all those who helped make this book a living reality. Your gift of time and love will bless others and help heal the hurts of many.

Thank you.
Brian L. Bohrer

Your 12
Personal Declarations

I refuse to allow my past to control my future.

I refuse to die within, when I can live.

I refuse to be the way that I am, when I can
be something better.

I refuse to allow money to make me into
something that I'm not.

I refuse to allow what someone else has done
to me, to cause me to do evil to others.

I refuse to be called dysfunctional, when
God created me to be fully functional.

I refuse to stay discouraged any longer,
when I can have peace and joy.

I refuse to remain bound, when I am
created to be free.

I refuse to stay at the bottom, when I
belong at the top.

I refuse to speak words of defeat, when
I can speak words of freedom.

I refuse to lose, when I know that I can win.

I refuse to remain sick, when I can recover.

Brian Bohrer Ministries • P. O. Box 1577 • Washington, MO 63090 (636) 239-5944

Contents

Foreword

> For I will restore health unto thee, and I will heal thee of thy wounds, saith the Lord.
>
> Jeremiah 30:17 KJV

FAITH BEGINS where the will of God is known. God said, "I will" restore. God is in the restoration business. When everyone else thinks your life is all over and ready for the junkyard, God says, "I will restore." When God restores, He does not just bring something back to its original condition; He makes it better than it ever was before. He restores souls (Psalm 23:3). He restores joy (Psalm 51:12). He restores years (Joel 2:25).

God has the parts to restore any human condition. As the Creator, He can make new parts. He restores bodies, minds, families, and finances. We are living in days of supernatural restoration.

> Behold, I will bring it health and cure, and I will cure them, and will reveal unto them the abundance of peace and truth.
>
> Jeremiah 33:6 KJV

Again, God's Word is "I will." We cannot question God's willingness or desire to restore and make us whole. God's Word is God's will. The Bible is God talking to you.

> And, behold, there came a leper and worshipped him, saying, Lord, if thou wilt, thou canst make me clean. And Jesus put forth his hand, and touched him, saying, I will, be thou clean. And immediately his leprosy was cleansed.
>
> Matthew 8:2,3 KJV

The man with leprosy did not question the ability of Jesus, He questioned His will. Jesus settled the question of the will of God forever and for everyone. He said, "I will." Other translations say: "Of course I want to" (*Jerusalem Bible*). "It is my pleasure" (*Basic English*). "I am desiring it with all my heart" (*Wuest*). It is the will of God for you to be healed and restored. That is the beginning of faith.

> He sent his word, and healed them, and delivered them from their destructions.
>
> Psalm 107:20 KJV

There is healing and restoration in the Word of God. The Word is full of life and power. As we feed on the Word, the healing power of God flows in us.

> But unto you that fear my name shall the Sun of righteousness arise with healing in his wings; and ye shall go forth, and grow up as calves of the stall.
>
> Malachi 4:2 KJV

The Sun of righteousness is the new day of redemption that is ours in Christ Jesus. Jesus took our infirmities, griefs, sorrows, shame, iniquities, transgressions, sicknesses, and poverty. On the cross He took our place and was made a curse for us. He died our death. On the third day He rose from the dead to give us righteousness, life, peace, healing, and blessing. The "Sun of Righteousness" has arisen and there is healing in His "beams."

In the light of redemption there is healing for everyone. The effect is like calves being released from the stall leaping for joy. We are coming out of the stall into new territory. We are going places we have never been and seeing things we have never seen.

In this book, *Winning on the Inside,* Pastor Brian Bohrer thoroughly shows God's willingness to restore and explains from his own personal testimony what God has done in his life. I know this book will be a blessing to many that others thought were losers and God turned into winners.

Mark Hankins
Alexandria, Louisiana

Introduction
Where do you go from here?

HAVE YOU GIVEN UP ON LIFE? Has your dream died? Have you been hurt by those you love or trust? Have you had a devastating experience? Maybe you wanted your life to be like those on "Little House on the Prairie." You may be wondering, like Humpty Dumpty, "How do I pick up the pieces?" This book will help you turn things around in your life and get back on the right course. This book is not about denial but about freedom over the pain that life throws your way.

Pain is a real thing that we all have to deal with. Some deal with it differently than others. Some ask questions like, "Why did this happen to me? I am a good person. Why do bad things happen to good people?" Well, once you find out "why" you are still left dealing with the fact that it did happen and the question, "Where do I go from here?"

This book is about finding your way back and the road that leads to true freedom. You can recover if you want to. The sad thing is, if a person does not get healed from what has happened to them, they will be one of the walking wounded.

The fact is, in life you will have the opportunity to get hurt. Hurt is the game of life. I have heard it said before that "life is not fair, but God is good!" Learning to conquer such things like disappointment, discouragement, despair, bitterness, and failure is the key to living above the pain that is in the world.

Life was made to win, and you can win and conquer the things that try to control and keep you in bondage. Your life is valuable—so valuable to God that He has a plan for you. The plan of God begins when you embrace facts from God's Word. Winning begins in life the moment you begin to win on the inside. Winning on the inside will allow you to win over the things that try to control you on the outside. No one or no thing can control you or keep you in bondage as long as you are free on the inside.

As a pastor for twenty-eight years, I've seen many people overcome pain in their lives. These people have won over the hurt of the death of loved ones; broken relationships; severe illness, both physical and mental; and from the pain of the past. Whatever you are facing, you are not the only one. Don't be fooled into thinking that your problem is so unique that nobody has gone through what you are going through.

This book is about a journey out of the pit of despair and self-pity. You may have been devastated by something in your life, but I know God will repair and restore all the areas in your life and deliver you out to complete wholeness.

One of my favorite statements from the Word of God is, **"Forgetting those things which are behind and reaching forward to those things which are ahead"** (Philippians 3:13). You can do it. Winning is the nature that abides within your inner being. Winning is moving forward and not allowing things that have happened to you, to happen through you!

Now, let's get ready to win.

Winning on the Inside

WINNING IS MOVING FORWARD AND NOT ALLOWING THINGS THAT HAVE HAPPENED TO YOU, TO HAPPEN THROUGH YOU!

Chapter 1

Leave the Past Behind

I refuse to allow my past to control my future.

He sent His word and healed them, and delivered them from their destructions.

Psalm 107:20

HAVE YOU BEEN SEARCHING for freedom from the inward pain and the hurts that life has dealt you? Have you been looking for help but you don't know where to find it? Have you been to counselors, therapists, and professionals to see if they can help relieve the anger and the hurt that lie within you? Have you ever said, "I will never be happy again, I will never find what I am looking for in life, or why does my life always turn out this way"?

There's hope for you! You are not alone. Many have been down the same road and have recovered. They have made it back to the top to enjoy life to the fullest. You can make it back. The journey may seem to be uphill. The road may be rough, but with the help of God you can make it. The fact is simple: If you keep everything buried within you, you will live your life in bondage. Hidden secrets keep you sick. God heals only what you reveal.

Some simple keys that lead to healing are:

1. *Finding* the road to recovery.

2. *Staying* on that road until you are completely healed.

You can do it! We will point you to the road. We will take you right up to the road, but it is up to you to stay on it. Remember this fact from *The Amplified Bible,* "**[I will] not in any degree leave you helpless nor forsake nor let [you] down...**" (Hebrews 13:5). Today is a new day. It's not a day to hide behind your past. It's a day to leave your past behind!

Winning on the Inside

HIDDEN SECRETS KEEP YOU SICK.
GOD HEALS WHAT YOU REVEAL!

Winning Over Bitterness

God's Word contains a plan for winning in every area of your life—including a plan to win over bitterness and the pain of the past. The entire Bible is about winning. Although the Bible tells how some losses occurred, it does so to show you "how" to win. God wants to make a winner out of you! And He wants you healed, restored, and whole.

In Jeremiah, chapter 30, verse 17, the prophet Jeremiah said:

> "For I will restore health to you and heal you of your wounds," says the Lord, "because they called you an outcast."

In this verse, **"I will restore health to you,"** refers to restoring health to your physical body. It is the will of God for your earthly, physical, natural body to be healed. In fact, 3 John 2 says, **"Beloved, I pray that you may prosper in all things and be in health, just as your soul prospers."**

How you feed upon the Word of God will affect your outward body, because God's Word contains healing medicine. We thank God for doctors who practice medicine (although the word *practice* bothers me). We believe God has given medicine and technological advances for our health. Also, according to Proverbs 4:22, God's Word is as medicine to all your flesh. It contains healing power for your body, as well as for your soul—which is made up of your mind, will, and emotions.

Did you know that people can also get sick in their soul? Sickness in the soul will affect the outward body. Jeremiah is saying, "Not only will I restore health to you, but I will also **heal you of your wounds.**" I believe this refers to your inner life, because wounds gather in your mind and memory.

The wounds here were caused by REJECTION: **"Because they called you an OUTCAST..."** (Jeremiah 30:17). God promises healing for all the wounds caused by rejection in your life. **"He gathers together the OUTCASTS [the rejected].... He heals the brokenhearted and binds up their wounds"** (Psalm 147:2,3).

Now let's look at Jeremiah 33:6:

Behold, I will bring it [your life][1] health and healing; I will
heal them and reveal to them the abundance of peace and truth.

If you have the life of God abiding on the inside of your
spirit, it will impart healing power and health to your soul and
body. God's will is that you walk on the path of divine health
and be emotionally sound.

My Healing

God's plan is much bigger than ours. God has a way
of delivering His people out of the deepest pit. Although
Attention Deficit Disorder (A.D.D.) is now widely recog-
nized, when I was a child it was not a common diagnosis. My
mother, along with my teachers, knew that something was not
right with me. Despite efforts to have me treated by doctors,
counselors, and specialists, I was not diagnosed with any such
disorder.

Monkey Boy

My mother knew something was wrong and it went
deeper than a minor hearing problem or A.D.D. During my
adolescence (ages 8 to 11), the night was a fearful time for my
family and me. While asleep, I would get up and run around
the house saying, "Something is wrong, I am falling." Then
I would finish my nighttime routine by acting like a monkey.

During the day at school I could not comprehend what
was going on in the classrooms. It seemed that I had what
Volcano Joe had in the movie, "a brain cloud." Far behind
my classmates, I was not a strong reader. When obeying my
teacher's request to read aloud, one of the guys yelled out,

"Hey, speed read!" My nickname from that day forward was thus born.

Special Learning Class

It wasn't long until I ended up in a special learning class, away from the normal classmates. How embarrassed and ashamed of myself I was! I knew that I had let my family down. While they were taking our class pictures, I even tried to hide myself by holding a book up over my face so no one would see me. It was almost too much for me to handle. I had gone from monkey boy to Mr. Speed Read into special learning class.

Then, a divine appointment was made. In 1972, having learned of my condition, Alvin and Anna Ruth Barker invited my family to join them on a trip to Tulsa. They were going to hear a woman preacher named Kathryn Kuhlman, who was conducting a miracle crusade.

I had never heard of Kathryn Kuhlman. I was just going for the ride. But I almost drove them crazy on the trip. I remember sitting in the front seat on the arm console between Alvin and my father. Never still or quiet for a moment, I asked them questions and talked out loud for the entire six-hour trip. One thing for sure, no one got sleepy in those days when I was around.

After arriving in Tulsa, we visited Oral Roberts University where the Barker's son, Ken, was a student. We then checked into a motel and joined thousands of others in the huge coliseum where Kathryn Kuhlman was speaking. All I remember is that I grew restless. After about one hour, I got up and began walking up and down, up and down, up and down the aisle. The meetings were several hours long, so I spent my time playing and running. Then, something happened.

He Touched Me

As I was running up and down the aisle, a hand gently touched the back of my neck. Suddenly, the whole room went into slow motion and its occupants disappeared. Kathryn Kuhlman and I were alone—I, in the balcony, and she, on the platform. She said, "There is someone up in the far side who has been tormented in his emotions. Jesus is healing you right now." When I looked at Kathryn, her eyes seemed to focus on mine. She was talking straight to me. It was like no one else could hear her. No one else was in the room.

At that time in my life, I did not recognize the Hand. I remember running excitedly to my mother and crying, "Something happened to me!" Caught up in the service herself, she didn't notice me. Everyone seemed to be charged with the presence of God. People around us were shouting "Amen!" By the time we got home, however, my mother sensed something was different in me. I talked continually about the service.

Now, more than twenty years later, I have become more familiar with the Hand of God. While praying or preaching I often become aware of that same gentle Hand on my neck. I sometimes feel the heat of God's touch and usually the healing anointing flows and God leads me to pray for the sick.

During that day long ago with Kathryn Kuhlman, the healing process began in my life. God's healing power is still at work in my life. Healing is a process, in many cases; we must walk it out by faith daily. God will do the same for you and for your children. God honors faith. As you believe in Him, He will honor your faith. Your healing miracle can begin today.

Jeremiah 33:6 AMP says:

> I will lay upon it [you] health and healing, and I will cure them [you] and will reveal to them [you] the abundance of peace (prosperity, security, stability) and truth.

God is saying, "I will impart health and wholeness to your life. I will cure you of your pain." In order to fulfill the plan of God upon your life, you must be whole and cured of the hurt and pain of life. Wounded, rejected, victimized people cannot fulfill the plan of God.

Winning on the Inside

YOUR HEALING MIRACLE
CAN BEGIN TODAY!

Jesus, Our Therapist

The fact is, most people need a therapist. The best One I know personally is Jesus. Jesus is our therapist. A therapist is one who treats a sickness or disability. Jesus is the One who took our sicknesses and gave us supernatural ability where we had lack. His words are therapeutic, having the power to heal and cure. In the Old Testament, God revealed Himself to the children of Israel as Jehovah Rapha, which is the Lord that healeth thee and the Lord our Physician. I like to say it this way, "Jehovah Rapha, the Lord, our therapist." Our therapist has every answer to solve life's problems.

God's Word goes on to say, "I will reveal to you the abundance of peace, the abundance of prosperity, the abundance of security, the abundance of stability and truth. I'm going to lay health and healing upon you." That's better than destruction, lightning bolts, and tornadoes!

The world tends to blame bad things that happen on God. For example, tornadoes, earthquakes, floods, and storms of destruction are called "acts of God." On the contrary, God is a good God. **"Every good gift and every perfect gift is from above..."** (James 1:17). He wants to bless you. God has an abundance of prosperity for you in every area of your life.

Thou Shalt Not Sweat It!

In heaven there is no lack. Jesus taught us, **"Your will be done on earth as it is in heaven"** (Matthew 6:10). Worry and fear are two of the self-inflicting wounds that man enjoys at a high price. My wife and I often remind each other that the eleventh commandment is, "Thou shalt not sweat it!" The Bible tells us, **"Casting all your care upon Him, for He cares for you"** (1 Peter 5:7).

The Amplified Translation of this verse says:

> Casting the whole of your care [all your anxieties, all your worries, all your concerns, once and for all] on Him, for He cares for you affectionately, and cares about you watchfully.

Today we live in a world where many people are experiencing anxiety attacks and they're coming apart at the seams because of stress, strife, and division. The Bible says, **"Whatever is not from faith is sin"** (Romans 14:23). When you enter into worry, you become one of the biggest sinners in the church! We know that immorality is sin; we agree it is bad and very evil. But worry is sin also.

God is concerned about wholeness in your mind, will, and emotions as much as He is concerned about your physical wholeness and well-being.

Gilead—A Place of Therapy

Go up to Gilead and take [the] balm. . . .

Jeremiah 46:11

So what should you do if you have been wounded and you are dealing with bitterness? Or if you need to be refreshed and restored from an attack against your soul? The Bible says one solution is to go up to Gilead! Gilead is a place of therapy for your inner hurts, a place of restoration. David realized that when he said, "**He restoreth my soul . . . for his name's sake**" (Psalm 23:3 KJV).

Gilead also means an eternal spring—a stream that is perpetual and will never run dry. Some have defined Gilead as a place of refreshing through worship. The balm is a type of medication and healing ointment. In Jeremiah 8:22 the prophet said, "**Is there no balm in Gilead?**" Today we can answer the prophet's question, "Yes, there is healing therapy for you in Gilead."

If you and I want to win over bitterness and the pain of the past, we must go up to Gilead and take our medicine. In other words, we need to get into the presence of the Lord through prayer, worship, and spending time with Him. God dwells in the praises of His people. In the presence of the Lord there is healing for the brokenhearted and wounded.

In order for you to go up to Gilead, you must leave the past behind. Gilead is an upward, forward place, while your past is a backward and downward place. Your past could be your worst enemy. God wants to set you free from the pain, abuse, hurts, and wounds of your past. He wants to set you free from the pain of broken relationships. If you're not healed and free from the past, you will become bitter. God wants you to go up to Gilead and take your medicine.

Psalm 107:20 AMP says, "**He sends forth His word and heals them and rescues them from the pit and destruction.**" The Word has healing power in it to deliver and rescue you from your destructions. It's not the will of God for you and me to self-destruct by allowing the root of bitterness to seep in and breed within us. If not stopped, bitterness will continue to grow within us, then rise up and conquer us.

God has a plan to teach us how to win over bitterness and the pain of the past. His plan is for us to leave the past behind. His plan is revealed to us in His Word. Let us go up to Gilead, a place of therapy, and receive our help.

Winning on the Inside

WHERE YOU ARE IS NOT AS
IMPORTANT AS WHERE
YOU ARE GOING!

Chapter 2

Bitterness, an Inward Dying

I refuse to die within when I can live.

I shall not die, but live, and declare the works of the Lord.

Psalm 118:17

BITTERNESS IS AN INWARD DYING process from a broken or wounded heart that eats away on the inside of a person. It is a soul problem. The soul—which is your mind, will, and emotions—can become so fragmented by the world that you begin to accept a victim mentality. Such a mentality will cause you to walk around saying, "I'm a victim of life." You cannot walk in freedom as long as you are calling yourself a victim. You're either a victim or a victor. But you can't be both.

Victim Mentality

You have to change your mentality. Let God, the author and finisher of your faith, bring you to a place where you can confidently say, "I am a victor. I'm no longer a victim, and

I'll not be a victim. I refuse to be a hurt person, because hurt people hurt people."

Many people watch TV talk shows, which have become popular in recent years. They identify with the anger of the victimized guests on these shows and conclude, "I am one of them. I'm one of the walking wounded." You don't have to be one of the walking wounded. You don't have to live your life locked up on the inside. Many people are not locked up outwardly but they are locked in a prison inwardly—a prison of anger and unresolved hurt. Jesus has the key to unlock the doors to your life. The question is, "Will you let Him in?"

Loss of Desire

Proverbs 13:12 says, **"Hope deferred makes the heart sick, but when the desire comes, it is a tree of life."** A bitter heart will cause a person to lose the desire to carry out what God has called them to do. And if it is not dealt with, a bitter person may even lose his or her desire to live. You must realize that your life is valuable to God and that He has a plan for you.

Philippians 2:13, *Weymouth's Translation,* says, **"It is God Himself whose power creates within you the desire to do His gracious will and also brings about the accomplishment of the desire."**

Broken Relationships

People become bitter through broken relationships, betrayal, divorce, separation, or disappointment in someone they have loved or trusted. Some people may even become bitter when a loved one dies. We must make bitterness a bridge to God, not a barricade to keep us from Him. I remember hearing Kenneth Copeland say, "When you miss it or when you sin, don't run from God. Run to Him." I never have forgotten that statement. So when you get bitter, don't hide from God. Run to Him!

Winning on the Inside

"WHEN YOU MISS IT OR WHEN YOU SIN, DON'T RUN FROM GOD. RUN TO HIM!"

Offenses

Other people become bitter because of offense. You will have many opportunities to be offended—in the world, in relationships, and even in the church. But don't take the opportunity to be offended. The Bible says if you love God's Word, you will not be offended (Psalm 119:165). *The King James Version* says, **"Nothing shall offend them."** There comes a point in your walk with God when you must choose whether to love God's Word or to pay the high price of taking offense.

Abuse

Abuse is another cause of bitterness. When a person doesn't know how to deal with abuse, they become bitter and walk around all their life with this oozing inward sore. It affects them in the workplace, and in personal relationships—especially in their marriage.

Abuse comes in many ways from childhood to adulthood. Obviously, if you want to be one of the walking wounded all your life, you have sufficient opportunity. But if you want to be healed and recover, you also have that choice. One sure way to keep your hurtful past alive is by telling everyone how others have abused you. There comes a day to grow beyond the pain of the past and to quit telling everybody about it. What I am trying to say is: Quit focusing on your hurts. Let them go. Don't tell another person. Put them behind you, under the blood of Jesus, and press on ahead.

Healing begins when we quit speaking about the past and begin to speak the promises of God. It's time to quit speaking about our past experiences and to start talking about our expectations for the future based on God's Word and redemption promises.

Winning on the Inside

HEALING BEGINS WHEN WE QUIT SPEAKING ABOUT THE PAST AND BEGIN TO SPEAK THE PROMISES OF GOD!

Mistreatment

Mistreatment is another opportunity to open the door to bitterness. Whenever you talk over and over again about how much you've been mistreated—whether through childhood trauma, misunderstanding, or miscommunication, you open the door to bitterness. Whenever you start feeling sorry for yourself, you are inviting the devil to come on in. You risk making a huge blaze out of a small bonfire. Remember this, anytime you are feeling sorry for yourself, you give the devil an opportunity to plant and water seeds of bitterness inside you.

When I was a young boy, I tried to repair a relative's lawn mower. I took it completely apart. I'll admit, I didn't really know what I was doing. But this man told me it was broken, and I thought I would try to fix it. I had removed the cover, the flywheel, the coil, and the piston. When he saw his mower in this condition, he asked, "What are you doing?" I said, "I'm fixing your lawn mower." He said to me, "No, you're not. You don't know what you are doing. Everything you touch turns to doo-doo!"

I went home after the incident saying, "Everything I touch turns to doo-doo." We laugh about it now, but this came from a relative I respected. His words set a boundary and a limitation on me. I never forgot what he said. I failed to realize that it was a mental block in my life until the Holy Ghost brought it up to me one day and said, "Right there is a problem." I felt I had been mistreated. But after I realized it was a problem, I dealt with it. God helped me to let it go.

They Called Me "Oral Roberts"

Persecution, if not handled properly, can be an open door to bitterness. But if we keep our hearts pure, God can use us to reach those who persecute us.

When I was nineteen years old, I was working at Brown & Root Construction Company in Ashdown, Arkansas, building a paper mill for Georgia-Pacific. This was my summer job to make money to go to school. I had already attended one year of Bible College in Houston, Texas, and I was getting ready to move to Tulsa for my second year.

Every morning I drove from Magnolia, Arkansas, to Ashdown for work. Most of the men on the construction site were not Christians—and at least initially, they didn't care too much for those who were. The workers were each assigned to different crews, and each crew was made up of what I like to call heathen "good ole boys." I can fairly call someone a "good ole boy," because as a Magnolia native, I was one myself. I guess these men saw me as some "pure" guy, so they began to harass me.

My crew members asked me, "What are you doing here?" I replied that I was working to get money so I could go to school. They asked, "What school are you going to attend?" I knew not to tell them, so I said, "I'm just going to college." They insisted, "Where?" I held back, "In Tulsa, Oklahoma." They nailed me, "What's the name of it?" I finally answered, "Rhema." They said, "We've never heard of Rhema. What type of school is it?" I didn't want to lie, so I admitted, "It's a school that teaches faith, a Bible school." They said, "Like Oral Roberts?" I said, "Yeah, like Oral Roberts." That was at the beginning of the summer—the beginning of a full summer of daily persecution in my life.

The next day when I walked into work in front of everyone a man yelled out, "Here comes Oral Roberts." Everybody turned to look at me, and they all began to laugh. They began to call me "Oral" at every turn. When I went to the snack shop, when I asked for a hammer or a nail, when clocking in and clocking out, I heard: "Hey, Oral. What have you been doing, Oral? Where are you going, Oral? Do you have any miracles for me today, Oral? Ladies and gentlemen, here comes Oral." They just didn't say "Oral," they said "Orrraaaall." So after several weeks of misery, I told my mother that I was quitting. She said, "No, you're not. We're going to pray for them."

After I had worked there about two months, the name calling had quieted down. I was on break with about thirty people gathered around—all of them heathen—and someone said, "Hey, Oral, why don't you heal Grady?" Grady was one of my co-workers who dipped snuff and spit his juice on my boots. I didn't want to pray for Grady. I was kind of glad that he wasn't feeling well. Then one of the men asked Grady, "What's wrong with you today?" Grady said, "I've got bursitis." Then mockingly, Grady pulled off his welder's cap and said to me, "Can you heal me, Oral?"

At nineteen I didn't know a whole lot, so I said, "Sure I will." I laid my hand on his head and said, "Be healed." God is my witness. The man fell to his knees and got up totally healed. He jumped back and said, "What did you do to me, Oral?" I said, "I didn't do anything to you." Grady said, "I felt something going out of your hand, you shocked me." That was the first of many miracles for the summer.

The second miracle happened when another co-worker asked me to pray for his wife. He offered, "If you come home with me to pray for Martha, I'll fix you a steak dinner. And you can spend the night." I asked him what was wrong with his wife. He answered, "She's eight months pregnant." I said, "There's nothing wrong with that." He said, "She is carrying twins and they are breach."

I didn't even know what breach meant at the time, but I didn't think it would be much of a problem. After all, God had already healed Shady Grady. I didn't know better than to pray. When you are young, you have reckless faith. You will pray for anything and everything, you even pray for a parking spot at Wal-Mart. I told my mother where I would be going, and I took one of Kenneth Hagin's books with me, called *What Faith Is.* I was off on my first missionary journey.

After we enjoyed a steak dinner (missionary food), and right before we went to bed, he said, "I want you to pray for my wife now." I laid hands on her and prayed in the name of Jesus. Then we went to bed.

Since it was near the end of summer, I soon went to Oklahoma for school. I began thinking about this couple, so I called them and asked the husband, "How are things with your wife?" He replied, "The strangest thing happened. The week before she delivered, the babies turned miraculously." Then he added, "Oral, I sure appreciate you coming and praying for her." (He didn't know my name wasn't Oral!)

God was able to turn what started out as persecution into a great blessing! Remember, if you don't get bitter, God will turn hard times into a blessing!

Why is it so important to identify bitterness and deal with it? If bitterness is allowed to grow, it will:

1. *Hinder your spirit.* Your spirit (inner man)— armored with faith and the Word of God—can help you rise above bitterness, the pain of the past, and bodily pain. The condition of your spirit will determine your outcome. Keep your inner man strong by praying in the Spirit and speaking the Word of God.

   Proverbs 18:14 says, **"The spirit of a man will sustain him in sickness, but who can bear a broken spirit?"** *The Amplified Translation* of this verse says, **"The strong spirit of a man sustains him in bodily pain or trouble,** but a weak and broken spirit who can raise up or bear?"

2. ***Rob you of your joy.*** Joy is an inward strength that comes from your inner man. Joy comes from fellowship with the Lord. Joy is heaven's remedy for end-time heaviness.

Nehemiah 8:10 says, **"The joy of the Lord is your strength."** *The Amplified Translation* of this verse says, **"Be not grieved and depressed, for the joy of the Lord is your strength and stronghold."**

3. ***Drain the river of God's life.*** In order for you to be strong, you must have an influx of God's flowing river. Bitterness will try to dam up the river of God. Prayer is the key to keep the river of God flowing into your life.

John 7:37,38 says, **"If anyone thirsts, let him come to Me and drink. He who believes in Me, as the Scripture has said, out of his heart will flow rivers of living water."**

John 10:10 says, **"The thief does not come except to steal, and to kill, and to destroy. I have come that they may have life, and that they may have it more abundantly."**

4. ***Paralyze your effectiveness for God.*** You cannot be effective for God as long as you allow bitterness to rule and reign in your life.

Proverbs 17:22 says, **"A merry heart does good, like medicine, but a broken spirit dries the bones."**

Many sicknesses can be traced back to bitterness and unforgiveness in a person's life. It dries up the bones and causes such diseases as arthritis, blood problems, and body deterioration.

Bitterness must be destroyed. If you don't destroy bitterness, it will destroy you. In the next chapter, we will discover the help that is available from God's presence to break the bondage of bitterness in your life.

Winning on the Inside
WHERE YOU ARE IS NOT AS IMPORTANT AS WHO YOU ARE!

Chapter 3

Changed By His Presence

*I refuse to be the way that I am when I
can be something better.*

Why are you cast down, O my inner self? And why should
you moan over me and be disquieted within me? Hope in God
and wait expectantly for Him, for I shall yet praise Him, Who is
the help of my countenance, and my God.

Psalm 42:11 AMP

I F WE ARE GOING TO WIN over bitterness and the
pain of the past, we need the presence of God moving in our lives. In His presence, we move beyond the
natural realm of reasoning, pain, hurt, and discouragement,
and step over into a higher realm of faith, healing, love, and
encouragement. In the presence of God there is healing for
bitterness and freedom from being brokenhearted.

Jesus said that He was anointed to set those free who were
oppressed and broken by life. The same anointing is available
today. The Word of God has the anointing of God abiding
within. What Jesus said about the anointing and the Holy
Spirit is still true today.

Jacob's Encounter

Jacob had a supernatural encounter in God's presence. Verse 12 of Genesis, chapter 28, says, **"Then he dreamed, and behold, a ladder was set up on the earth, and its top reached to heaven...."** That's shouting ground!

When you need help today, I have good news for you: There's a ladder that God can send down from heaven to touch the ground. I'm glad the ladder comes all the way to the ground, because God is the Great Physician who comes to our aid when we get low. I'm glad God didn't say, "Now, make it on your own." There is help from heaven in this very hour. I'm interested in getting on that ladder. How about you? God, Jesus, the Holy Spirit, and angels descend on that ladder, not to level you down and low but to bring you up and out.

Bethel: An Awesome Place

In Jacob's dream, he saw the angels of God **"ascending and descending on it"** (Genesis 28:12). I'm glad they were not just ascending, because here in the earth is where we need the help. Right where you are now, God is sending His anointing to deliver you. The angels of God have been sent to help us.

> The angel of the Lord encamps all around those who fear Him, and delivers them...The righteous cry out, and the Lord hears, and delivers them out of all their troubles. The Lord is near to those who have a broken heart, and saves such as have a contrite spirit. Many are the afflictions of the righteous, but the Lord delivers him out of them all.
>
> Psalm 34:7,17-19

Upon awaking from sleep after Jacob's encounter with God he said, **"Surely the Lord is in this place..."** (Genesis 28:16). Verse 17 says, **"And he was afraid and said, 'How awesome is this place!'"**

Jacob described the presence of God as "an awesome place." There are no words to describe the presence of God, but *awesome* comes close. If you saw a ladder come down to the earth from heaven with angels ascending and descending, you wouldn't sit there like a bump on a log. You'd say, "Glory to God! This is an awesome place!"

Then Jacob went on to say, **"This is none other than the house of God..."** (Genesis 28:17). There's nothing like the dwelling place of God. When we gather together in the presence of God, things take place. The Bible says, **"For where two or three are gathered together in My name, I am there in the midst of them"** (Matthew 18:20).

Jacob said, **"This is none other than the house of God, and this is the gate of heaven!"** (Genesis 28:17). Jacob saw the very gate of heaven. We've heard about the windows of heaven, but we haven't heard much about the gate of heaven. The windows of heaven represent God's provision, but the gate of heaven represents God's power and the angelic ministry. As we gather to seek His face, His abiding presence comes to demonstrate heaven's goodness.

Verses 18 and 19 of Genesis, chapter 28, go on to say:

> Then Jacob rose early in the morning, and took the stone that he had put at his head, set it up as a pillar, and poured oil on top of it.
>
> And he called the name of that place Bethel....

Bethel is translated as "the house of God" or "the dwelling place of the Almighty." The Bible says Jacob rose early in the morning, and took the stone that he had put at his head, set it up as a pillar, poured oil over it, and dedicated that place to God. **"Then Jacob made a vow..."** (v. 20). A *vow* means "a covenant between two parties." It means "commitment." Jacob made a commitment of his life to God and he promised to give a tenth back to God of everything that He gave him. Jacob was a tither.

Making a Commitment to God

The commitment you make to God—and to being in His presence—will help you break bitterness in your life. Some people will commit to card clubs, community art clubs, bridge clubs, or to checkerboard clubs. Yet when it comes to being committed to God and to coming into His house of worship, these same people back off.

I have come across a few men who are committed to hunting. They carry a hunting license in their billfold. There's nothing wrong with hunting. Other men are committed to fishing, and they carry a fishing license with them. Some of these fishermen have a boat that is licensed. They have an old raggedy car that blows out blue smoke, and it has a license on the back of it. They have a hunting dog—full of ticks—in a pen in the backyard, and even the dog has a license.

Some of these same men want to live with a woman and never enter into a marriage covenant with her. They want the "rights" of marriage without a license! They call it common law living. They have a license for everything but marriage. Their problem is, they are committed to easy street.

Some men will say, "Baby, I really love you, but I don't know for sure if I'm ready to make the big commitment. I will do anything for you. These flowers are proof that I love you." They give flowers at funerals, too, ladies! That's not a commitment to anything but your body!

They will tell you all of that just to get you to go to bed so they can brag to their friends, "Look what I've done." They've got their shirt buttoned down three buttons with five hairs poking out! They have used mascara on these five hairs to cover the gray, and they have gold chains around their neck. Ladies, you want someone who is committed to God, someone who will say, "Let's eat out after we get through praying at the church on Saturday night." Instead of going to the lake on Sunday, one who will be committed to going to church with you.

The vow Jacob was speaking about was more than lip service. He made a commitment to God. He said:

> If God will be with me, and keep me in this way that I am going, and give me bread to eat and clothing to put on,
>
> So that I come back to my father's house in peace, then the Lord shall be my God.
>
> And this stone which I have set as a pillar shall be God's house, and of all that You give me I will surely give a tenth to You.
>
> Genesis 28:20-22

The commitment you make to God is key. Many people are bitter because they have come out of a relationship just like I described. They have been burned by a broken, selfish relationship. Many times wounded people will hunt down wounded people and enter into a relationship with them because misery loves company.

This is the importance of the presence of the Lord that Jacob was speaking about, because when you come to the presence of God, you will find people in the process of being healed and made whole. They are on the potter's wheel. The Master's hands are upon their life and they're going through transformation. They're not perfect, but they're on the potter's wheel to be healed and restored. They desire to come out on the other side.

Jacob was saying to the Lord, "My commitment is toward You and Your house, because Your commitment is toward me." Jacob made a vow to God that everything God blessed him with, he would give Him a tenth. Jacob went on to do what God called him to do. But later in Genesis, we see the need for Jacob to return to Bethel, the presence of the Lord for a second touch.

Second Touch!

The key to winning over bitterness and leaving your past behind is that you must return to the presence of the Lord. The first touch puts you on the right path. You may have clarity in your mind for a season, but the devil is faithful to try to creep back into your mind with thoughts of pain, wounds, and hurts of the past. The enemy's motive is to try to get bitterness to take up residence in you.

When bitterness tries to creep back into your life, anger will try to creep back in, too. The thing that you must do is run to God, not from Him. Go back to Bethel for a second touch, just as Jacob did.

Winning on the Inside

I WILL NO LONGER BE BITTER, WITH
GOD'S TOUCH I WILL BE BETTER!

When God Touched My Heart

I remember well one time when the Lord touched my heart and allowed me to see hurting and suffering people. I was eleven at the time when my pastor, Henry Pletcher, stopped by my house for a visit. I was sitting in my favorite chair, rocking my worries away. He said to me, "In the morning I am going to Mexico with a group of teenagers. Would you like to go?" I immediately said yes.

What faith my pastor had to take a kid like me to Mexico to work in an orphanage! Looking back, I see that God used taking me out of my American culture to fulfill His plan for my life. From the age of eleven until I graduated from high school, I spent part of each summer in Reynosa, Mexico, working with Brother Don Russell in the language school and in the orphanage.

Going to any developing country at a young age often prepares the heart for the move of God and what God wants to do in your life. I would encourage any young person to take a trip to a foreign country while they are still in their teens. It will be life changing.

Our problems seem small in comparison to those children who have no home, no shoes, and no food. When you consider those in prison or in some kind of rehab for their addiction, you will lift your voice to God and say, "Thank You, Lord, for working in my life." If it were not for grace, I would be there, too. If you are there, remember, God is your Deliverer.

God has a way of reaching and using people who normally would not be chosen by the church or society. God can use the most disqualified to reach others for Him. He is looking for someone who is willing and obedient to His voice. We see this in the life of Jacob, we see God's touch working in his life.

In Genesis 35, verse 1, God said, **"Arise, go up to Bethel and dwell there; and make an altar there to God...."** The altar of the Lord is a place of repentance, prayer, and worship. Verse 9 says, **"God appeared to Jacob again...."** In verse 10 God said, **"Your name shall not be called Jacob anymore, but Israel shall be your name."**

Change is painful, but change is profitable. You can't do what God has called you to do and you can't win over bitterness and over your past unless there is change. We are changed and we receive power to change from the presence of God, the same place where Jacob got it. We must be willing to go back to Bethel—into God's presence—for a second touch.

Moses' Encounter

Moses also had an unusual encounter with the presence of God. We read in Exodus 34:29-33, that when Pastor Moses came down from Mount Sinai, the deacons said to one another, "Hey, you are glowing in the dark." The Bible says, **"The skin of his face shone while he talked with Him. So when Aaron and all the children of Israel saw Moses, behold, the skin of his face shone, and they were afraid to come near him"** (vv. 29,30).

Moses had been with God. The presence and the anointing of the Lord were upon him that day in a mighty way. No doubt, he was changed by the glory of God. The glory of God will bring inward change that will have an effect on the outward appearance. Moses had to put a veil over his face so the children of Israel could look at him.

But we read an amazing fact about the New Covenant believer, how they are in a different class than the children of Israel. Second Corinthians 3:14 says, **"Their minds were blinded. For until this day the same veil remains unlifted in the reading of the Old Testament, because the veil is taken away in Christ."**

WOW! The veil is taken away in Christ. You may ask, "When is the veil taken away?" When one is born again. (You can find out how to be born again on page 141.)

> Whenever a person turns [in repentance] to the Lord, the veil is stripped off and taken away.
>
> Now the Lord is the Spirit, and where the Spirit of the Lord is, there is liberty (emancipation from bondage, freedom).
>
> And all of us, as with unveiled face, [because we] continued to behold [in the Word of God] as in a mirror the glory of the Lord, are constantly being transfigured into His very own image in ever increasing splendor and from one degree of glory to another; [for this comes] from the Lord [Who is] the Spirit.
>
> 2 Corinthians 3:16-18 AMP

More Glory in Christ

Moses had a certain degree of glory upon his life. This glory gave him influence and ability to lead the people. Now most of us would be satisfied with the glory that was on his life, but we actually possess a greater glory. This greater glory is found in Christ.

> The mystery which has been hidden from ages and from generations, but now has been revealed to His saints.
>
> To them God willed to make known what are the riches of the glory of this mystery among the Gentiles: which is Christ in you, the hope of glory.
>
> Colossians 1:26,27

Being *in Christ* and understanding that fact, gives you access to the glory that brings change to your life. The greater glory is found only *in Christ.* Once you understand who you are *in Christ* and what you have in Him, you will understand that the glory of Christ abides in your inner man.

Notice in the scripture below that we are partakers of the greater glory.

> Therefore, holy brethren, partakers of the heavenly calling, consider the Apostle and High Priest of our confession, Christ Jesus,
>
> Who was faithful to Him who appointed Him, as Moses also was faithful in all His house.
>
> For this One has been counted worthy of more glory than Moses, inasmuch as He who built the house has more honor than the house.
>
> For every house is built by someone, but He who built all things is God.

And Moses indeed was faithful in all His house as a servant, for a testimony of those things which would be spoken afterward,

But Christ as a Son over His own house, whose house we are if we hold fast the confidence and the rejoicing of the hope firm to the end.

Hebrews 3:1-6

Five things happen to you when you are under the influence of the glory:

1. You *hear* God's voice more clearly.

2. You *receive* revelation from God and His Word.

3. You get *direction* for your life.

4. You are *changed* by the presence of God.

5. The *healing process* begins.

Winning on the Inside

A NEW ENCOUNTER WITH GOD
WILL REQUIRE YOU TO MOVE
FORWARD WITH YOUR LIFE.

Chapter 4

A Seed Sown,
Not a Seed Stolen

*I refuse to allow money to make me into
something that I'm not.*

I have been young and now am old, yet have I not seen the
[uncompromisingly] righteous forsaken or their seed begging
bread.

Psalm 37:25 AMP

WHEN I WAS STARTING OUT as a young
preacher at the age of twenty, I had an opportunity to get bitter over money. Many people
get bitter over money.

I had gone to a small church in Louisiana to preach. There
were about eighty people there. I was excited because I had
broken the fifty people mark! I preached the gospel and did
everything I knew to do. I followed all the instructions that
I was taught to follow: I waved my hands, kicked my feet,
spit cotton, got my handkerchief out and waved it around, I
changed my voice.

I had said to the Lord about the offering, "Lord, You know my needs and the needs of my family. You know the bills that we have, and I believe tonight there will be plenty of provision."

At offering time, the pastor said, "We're going to take up an offering for the young evangelist." I had a friend sitting in the congregation. He pulled out his last $20 bill and said, "This is my last $20. I'm giving it to you." I said, "Thank you. I need that $20."

The offering plate was full. I said, "Glory to God! My bills are paid. My needs are supplied. I'm going to eat some steak. I'm tired of gospel bologna and cheese! I'm ready for some full gospel, Word of faith steak!"

At the end of the service, the pastor shook my hand and said, "That was a great message. We want you to come back and be with us." He gave me one of those apostolic handshakes. An apostolic handshake is when people come up to you and put an offering in your hand. Then you've got to be slick, smile, and slide the money into your pocket.

As I was driving home, I was whistling a new tune! My friend sitting in the backseat asked, "How much?" I got real spiritual: "Oh, brother, it's nobody's business but God's and mine." "How much was the offering, brother?" he insisted. "Let's go out and eat." "It's nobody's business but God's and mine. My needs are met."

I pulled the wad of money out of my pocket, handed it to my friend in the backseat, and I said, "Count it out, brother, and let's have a shouting service all the way home!"

So he began counting: "$5, $10, $15, $16, $17, $18, $19, $20. You got $20 in that offering." He said, "It's a miracle! I put a $20 bill in there and now it's three $5's and five $1's." That's not exactly the miracle I desired!

I got so angry I wanted to call the pastor. For weeks I talked about it and steamed over what he had done to me. I stewed in remembering his lying to the congregation, "This offering is for the evangelist." He had in fact kept most of that offering. Suddenly, I realized that something was creeping into my life: Bitterness was trying to take root in me.

Winning on the Inside

MONEY IS NOT THE MOST IMPORTANT THING IN LIFE; IT JUST ALLOWS YOU TO DO WHAT IS IMPORTANT!

Destroy It, Before It Destroys You

God said to me, "You'd better deal with that." I said, "But God, do You know what he did to me?" God said, "You'd better deal with it." I said, "But You don't know what he did to me." The human nature wants to plead your own case! We want to tell everybody what happened, and how we're mistreated. God said, "You'd better deal with that bitterness and anger, because if you don't destroy it, it will rise up and destroy you."

I wrestled with that thing and finally got control of it. I said, "God, I don't want to be a bitter preacher." There's nothing worse than a bitter preacher. He gets that growl in his voice and that look in his eyes. I said, "God, I want to be a happy preacher." He said, "If you want to keep on walking the path, you'd better get rid of the bitterness. Satan has sent it to derail you." I forgave the pastor of that church, but I also learned a lesson about money: Never allow money to control you.

Since that time, I've had many opportunities to win over bitterness in other areas of my life. With help from heaven, we can overcome every opportunity of getting bent out of shape. We can stay free of bitterness and win over the things in our past.

Winning on the Inside

PEOPLE WHO DON'T HAVE ANYTHING
IMPORTANT TO DO,
DON'T NEED ANY MONEY.

Lost Inheritance

Many people get hurt and separate over money and the loss of money. Many families have been destroyed over inheritances and the pain of bankruptcies. I know that it can be devastating to your life when you feel that you have been cheated and robbed. But God has a way of turning things around for the righteous. Here are a few tips:

Never allow greed to rule and stay in your life. Greed will cause you to do things that you would never do normally. Greed causes people to steal or embezzle, cheat on their taxes, and build walls of hatred and distrust, even to take another's life. Greed is a compulsion that must be destroyed before it destroys you and those you love. You never win by taking something that belongs to someone else. You never win when something has been taken from you and you don't forgive. When you feel like something has been taken from you, don't allow those evil emotions to become a monster of hate and revenge.

Winning on the Inside

PROSPERITY IS IMPORTANT, SO YOU
CAN DO WHAT IS IMPORTANT
FOR GOD.

Apply these principles when you feel that you have been cheated and robbed from something that belongs to you.

1.   *Give it to God and let Him fight your battles.*

For the battle is not yours, but God's.

2 Chronicles 20:15

For I will contend with him [or them] who contends with you, and I will save your children.

Isaiah 49:25

Our God has never lost a battle. When we give our battles to the Lord, it is an act of our faith. It is an act of His love working in our lives. Your flesh will desire to do evil to those people who have hurt and stolen from you, but we must give it to God and allow Him to take care of it.

God wants to bring you to the place that you do not desire evil to be done to those who have hurt you. You know that your deliverance and freedom are on the way when your heart sincerely wants blessings for those who have done you wrong.

2. *Call it a seed sown, not a seed stolen.*

When we were living in Louisiana, we pulled into the driveway after church one Sunday night. I noticed that my bicycle was missing. Now this was a top-of-the-line touring bike, and it was gone. I was mad and upset about it. After I complained to the Lord for several days, He said to me, "Do you want it to be a seed stolen, or do you want to make it a seed sown?"

That day the Lord taught me a lesson on how to get things out of my life that don't belong in me. I don't have to walk around hurt and upset. The Lord said, "You have a part to play if you want to turn things around. Making it a seed is the key, and it will return back to you." The law of seedtime and harvest will work in many situations. Proverbs 6:31 tells us that when the thief is found, he must restore sevenfold.

3. *Don't get bitter over your losses, God will restore.*

Bitterness shuts the door on the blessing of God. Bitter people are ungrateful people. What belongs to you will come back to you if you walk in love and forgiveness. God is a master on bringing people who have lost in life back to the top. The way back to the top is through the door of love and forgiveness.

> Even my own familiar friend [family members] in whom I trusted, who ate my bread, has lifted up his heel against me.
>
> But You, O Lord, be merciful to me, and raise me up.
>
> Psalm 41:9,10
>
> When the Lord brought back the captives [who returned] to Zion, we were like those who dream [it seemed so unreal].

Then were our mouths filled with laughter, and our tongues with singing. Then they said among the nations, The Lord has done great things for them.

The Lord has done great things for us! We are glad!

Turn to freedom our captivity and restore our fortunes....

Psalm 126:1-4 AMP

God will restore and raise you up as you walk in love and forgiveness. In the next chapter we will travel UP the road of forgiveness. Remember that recovery comes when you allow the power of forgiveness to work in your life.

Winning on the Inside
FORGIVENESS IS AN INVESTMENT INTO YOUR FUTURE.

Chapter 5

The Power of Forgiveness

I refuse to allow what someone else has done
to me to cause me to do evil to others.

Bless the Lord, O my soul; and all that is within me, bless His holy name!

Bless the Lord, O my soul, and forget not all His benefits:

Who forgives all your iniquities, who heals all your diseases.

Psalm 103:1-3

TO WIN OVER THE PAIN OF THE PAST, you must understand the *power of forgiveness*, which is always the first step toward recovery.

Forgiveness is not saying, "I forgive you, but I'll never forget." "I'll forgive you, but I'm going to bring it up every week." Or, "I forgive you, but I'm going to tell my closest friends." Forgiveness is putting the past behind you. It is walking in the love of God and not making a person pay for their mistakes. The power of forgiveness will work as medicine to your soul.

> ## Winning on the Inside
> FORGIVENESS IS PUTTING
> THE PAST BEHIND YOU

The Bridge to Wholeness

Forgiveness is a bridge to wholeness. Unforgiveness is a barricade. Unforgiveness and bitterness are roadblocks that will stop you from moving forward in life. Forgiveness is not a suggestion. It's a requirement, according to the Word of God. The Bible says, **"If you do not forgive, neither will your Father in heaven forgive your trespasses"** (Mark 11:26).

In your opinion, a person may not deserve forgiveness because of the horrible abuse and pain they have inflicted. But forgiveness is something that you really give yourself. When you release the wrongdoer, you have made a decision that you're not going to live a bitter life and be a bitter person. When you forgive and release someone, you are saying, "I'm forgiving them because I will not allow what they have done to control me and keep me a bitter person. I will not allow their mistake to dominate me for the rest of my life."

> ## Winning on the Inside
> FORGIVENESS IS A BRIDGE
> TO WHOLENESS.

Release Yourself

To release yourself from the bondage of bitterness is a choice that you make. Your end through forgiveness will be better than your beginning. The Bible says that God declares the end from the beginning (Isaiah 46:10). God has declared a new beginning in your life (Isaiah 43:18,19). God has not declared that we live our lives full of bitterness. Bitterness leaves an open door for every attack of the enemy.

The Bible says, "God heals the brokenhearted and binds up their wounds." Let's go to Gilead—the perpetual spring of God's peace—because there is medicine and recovery at Gilead. The Doctor is in twenty-four hours a day and He is making house calls. Jesus never told anyone to come back tomorrow or, "I don't have time." He has an opening for you TODAY!

As you apply the medicine of God's Word to your life, you will come out on the other side healed and whole with the joy of the Lord radiating from you.

The Holy Spirit spoke to my heart and said, "I don't want My people bitter and controlled by pain. I want My people to realize that they can go to Bethel, My presence, for a second touch. If you want to overcome bitterness and the pain of the past, it will take a second touch of My presence."

Winning on the Inside

YOUR END THROUGH FORGIVENESS
WILL BE BETTER THAN
YOUR BEGINNING!

Forgiveness the Size of Texas

Not long ago I watched a television program about three young men in Texas who killed a young girl. The saddest part of the story was, this young girl had trusted them because they were all friends.

This is a true story about the pain that is found in the world today. This story had an impact on my life for many days so I thought I would tell you a little about it.

One of the young men, now in prison, confessed his crime. He was broken by the realization of what he had done to the young girl and to her family who were left without a daughter to care for and love. The young man in prison asked if he could see the family to ask them to forgive him and to tell them that he was truly sorry. He seemed to have true repentance for what had happened.

But the biggest thing that made an impact upon my life was the attitude of the parents and their testimony on national television. The interviewer, Barbara Walters, asked the mom and the dad how they could go on with life after such a tragic thing had happened. This couple began to talk about the forgiveness of God. They described how bitterness almost tore their lives apart and made them into the same monster who destroyed their child. They openly shared how God had healed them and given them strength to forgive.

Hate will always produce more hate; bitterness will always produce more bitterness; and hurt people will always hurt more people. My heart went out to this couple as I listened to them talk about their pain. At the same time, I received strength from them as they talked about how God had dealt with them about forgiving. The healing process that they described that night was not a normal thing. It was a miraculous God working in their lives and the power of forgiveness ministering through them to others. I would not be a bit surprised if thousands across America struggling with unforgiveness during the program received strength to forgive and to move forward with their lives.

This mother and father are some of the strongest people that I have ever seen. Instead of hiding and burying themselves with hate and unforgiveness, they came out in public and shared their hurts and healing with others. Wow, what an incredible couple!

Winning on the Inside

FORGIVENESS PRODUCES A STRENGTH THAT NO ONE CAN TAKE FROM YOU.

There Is Hope

This couple is living proof that you can come out of the deepest pit, the darkest prison, if you allow God to work in your life. It may be painful at first, but it will get better. If we really understood what happens to us when we do not forgive others, we would learn to forgive for our own good. When we do not forgive we incarcerate ourselves. Unforgiveness does not imprison the one we do not forgive, it imprisons us. Don't punish yourself any longer by keeping unforgiveness in your life, release them and release yourself. God is your only hope. He can bring you out. He will give you the strength to forgive if you will only ask Him. You can do it!

Winning on the Inside

FORGIVENESS IS NOT WEAKNESS IN YOUR CHARACTER; IT IS A STRENGTH THAT BRINGS PROMOTION.

Chapter 6

Removing the Thorn

I refuse to be called dysfunctional, when
God created me to be fully functional.

For as the rain comes down, and the snow from heaven, and do not return there, but water the earth, and make it bring forth and bud, that it may give seed to the sower and bread to the eater,

So shall My word be that goes forth from My mouth; it shall not return to Me void, but it shall accomplish what I please, and it shall prosper in the thing for which I sent it.

Isaiah 55:10,11

THE SPIRIT OF GOD speaking through the prophet Isaiah was saying, "My Word is just like the water from heaven." He compared a natural law to a spiritual law. The natural law is the rain that causes the seed that's in the earth to bring forth, bud, and grow. Then He says, **"So shall My word be that goes forth from My mouth..."** (v. 11).

When the Word goes forth from His mouth, that is, it must become God speaking to you, it's just like the rain falling from heaven. Before you were ever born, God put seeds within you that will spring up as soon as the Word of God finds entrance into your heart. These seeds are your future; they are the seeds of greatness. The end to a painful season is the beginning of a fruitful life. Once you are ready to get on with your life, at that point the fruitful life begins.

Verse 11 says, "**It** [God's Word] **shall not return to Me void** [empty or powerless]...." The words that have been spoken to you will not return to you powerless. The Word has the power within itself to carry out God's full plan for wholeness in your life. What God said in His Word, He is going to do. He is not a man that He should lie (Numbers 23:19). He backs His Word. The promises of God that have been spoken over you, as well as His promises which you are speaking over yourself, will come to pass if you'll continue to water those seeds—believing them, speaking them, and acting upon them.

Winning on the Inside

THE END TO A PAINFUL SEASON
IS THE BEGINNING OF A FRUITFUL LIFE.

The Words of Your Mouth

The words of your mouth hold the key to God moving in your life. Line the words of your mouth up with what you are expecting, not with what you are experiencing. Many people want to talk about all the bad things they are experiencing, but you need to line your life up with what you are expecting to take place. The Bible is a book of expectation. God is waiting for you to take your stand and move forward. He will be there to guide you every step of the way.

Saying What God Says

What you say today and how you say it has everything to do with the direction of your life. Once you understand Proverbs 18:21, **"Death and life are in the power of the tongue...,"** you can steer your life in the right direction by speaking and saying what God's Word says about your life.

Words are very powerful and what you say today lives tomorrow. You can't keep saying the wrong things and expect God to bring deliverance to you. God moves on the wings of your words.

There comes a point in your walk with God, when God requires that you control what you say and think. In order to see the hand of God moving in your life, you must mature in being master of your tongue and mind.

You can't keep saying things like, "I am a failure," "Nothing works out for me," "I have messed up my life beyond repair." "I am a depressed person." "I am a dysfunctional person." "I am always lonely." "I will never be happy." As long as you keep saying statements like these, that's exactly what you will experience. You become what you say.

> ## Winning on the Inside
> IN ORDER TO SEE THE HAND OF GOD
> MOVING IN YOUR LIFE, YOU MUST
> MATURE IN BEING MASTER OF YOUR
> TONGUE AND MIND.

Your Identity

Once you learn what you should not say, you must go to the next level where you learn what you should say.

Your words form your identity, and your words are connected to your identity. As long as you keep saying that you are an alcoholic, you will be an alcoholic. Your words form an inner image within you, and your words are connected to who you are. What you have said in the past is what you have become today.

You will never enjoy the freedom that God wants you to have until you change your vocabulary and eliminate death from coming out of your mouth.

> ## Winning on the Inside
> YOUR WORDS FORM AN INNER IMAGE
> WITHIN YOU, AND YOUR WORDS ARE
> CONNECTED TO WHO YOU ARE.

Launch Yourself Forward

Your words will launch you into the plan of God. Once you understand the power of your words and that Mark 11:23 says you have what you say, you can get your words to work for you instead of having them work against you. You will tap into the ability of God when you begin to get God's Word in your mouth. **"This Book of the Law** [God's Word, God's power, God's ability, God's strength, God's healing, God's anointing, and God's deliverance] **shall not depart from your mouth..."** (Joshua 1:8).

Philemon, verse 6, tells us that "your faith will be effectual by the acknowledging of every good thing which is in you in Christ Jesus." *Acknowledge* means to believe, speak, declare, to admit as true, and to confess. You are to acknowledge who you are, what you have, and what you can do through Christ.

Winning on the Inside

UNDERSTANDING "WHO YOU ARE IN CHRIST" IS THE KEY TO PUTTING YOUR PAST IN ITS PROPER PLACE.

Dysfunctional—Began with Adam

No one was dysfunctional until the fall of man; I can picture Adam right after he ate of the fruit of the tree of knowledge of good and evil, turning to Eve and saying, "Now I am dysfunctional." Then I can picture Eve putting her hands on her hips and saying, "That's nothing. Now I am codependent."

Adam's disorder was passed down to you and me. Romans 5:12 tells us that Adam's sin brought death into the world and that death passed unto all men because all men were spoken for by Adam. The fall moved man from being dominated by his spirit to the realm of the intellect and reasoning which were dependent totally on his five senses.

Before the fall of man, Adam's spirit dominated his soul and his body. After the fall, Adam's soul began to dominate him and to give him trouble. Genesis 3:10 shows us that the first place fear showed up in the human race was right after the fall of man. Adam said, **"I was afraid."**

In Adam

When Adam sinned, this disorder fell to every man because all men came from Adam. Actually, when Adam sinned, you and I sinned with him because you and I were in the loins of Adam. You and I were in Adam.

> For [in Adam][2] all have sinned and fall short of the glory of God.
>
> Romans 3:23

Adam is your great, great, great, etc., great granddaddy. The results of his actions fell on you and me. When you were born into the world, what happened in the Garden became yours vitally and legally.

Functional—Began with Christ

You may say, "That's not fair!" It might not be fair if God had left us in that condition, but He didn't, thanks to Jesus. First Corinthians 15:45 tells us, "**…The first man Adam became a living being. The last Adam became a life-giving spirit.**" What the first Adam did affected every man with death and made man a dysfunctional living being. Christ being the last Adam, affected the spirit of man, bringing him back into fellowship and union with the Father.

When you were physically born, all that was true of Adam because of the fall, became true of you. You entered into your great grandfather Adam's inheritance: sin, sickness, poverty, death, dysfunctions, disorders, and Satan's dominion.

The same is true when you were born again spiritually. All that was true of Christ because of His death, burial, and resurrection is true in you. It belongs to you because of the new birth. You received and entered into your inheritance: victory over sin, victory over sickness, victory of poverty, victory over dysfunctions, victory over disorders, and victory over Satan's dominion.

In Christ

The believer is no longer in Adam, but in Christ. You are out of Adam and have disinherited all he sold you out to! You are in Christ and have inherited all He purchased for you! Adam sold you out to the slavery of the dominion of Satan, but Christ paid for and totally purchased your freedom and victory over your past.

> ## Winning on the Inside
> YOU ARE OUT OF ADAM AND HAVE
> DISINHERITED ALL HE SOLD
> YOU OUT TO!

As long as you see yourself in Adam, you will be part of his dysfunctional family, but the moment you see yourself in Christ, you become a part of His functional family who has victory over the disorders that are in the world. I like to say it this way: Jesus put the "FUN" in functional living.

> ## Winning on the Inside
> YOU ARE IN CHRIST AND HAVE
> INHERITED ALL HE PURCHASED
> FOR YOU!

Psychospeak Labels

In the world of psychology, professionals use "psychospeak labels,"[3] a vocabulary composed by psychological experts to describe human behavior. These labels are often presented in noun form: "an adult child," "an abused person," "an alcoholic," "codependent," "a foodaholic."

Today, "the mental health industry has over 292 different disorders, compared to 1917 when there were only 59 distinct forms of mental disorders."[4] As you can see we have really grown in our latest discoveries.

Many of these labels are often preceded by the confession, "I am…[this]…." As a person speaks and confesses these new-found discoveries, they are setting the boundaries upon their lives. One must never accept the role of a "dysfunctional label" unless they are willing to give up a part of their freedom, being limited by their words.

There is a connection to who you are and the words that come out of your mouth. Your words have formed your past, present, and they will form your future.

Proverbs 6:2 KJV says, **"Thou art snared by the words of thy mouth, thou art taken with the words of thy mouth."** *Basic English Translation* says, **"You are taken as in a net by the words of your mouth, the sayings of your lips have overcome you."** As you can see, it is very plain in this scripture and translation that your words and mouth have power to hold you in slavery.

Winning on the Inside

YOUR WORDS HAVE FORMED YOUR PAST, PRESENT AND THEY WILL FORM YOUR FUTURE.

Now notice these scriptures in the book of Proverbs and pay very close attention to the connection between your words and your life.

Wisdom in Proverbs

Proverbs 4:24 KJV - **Put away from thee a froward mouth, and perverse lips put far from thee.**

> *Moffatt's Translation - Bar out all talk of evil, and banish wayward words.*

Proverbs 10:19 KJV - **In the multitude of words there wanteth not sin: but he that refraineth his lips is wise.**

> *Good News Bible* - The more you talk, the more likely you are to sin....

> *Basic English* - ...he who keeps his mouth shut does wisely.

Proverbs 10:11 KJV - **The mouth of a righteous man is a well of life....**

Proverbs 12:6 KJV - **The words of the wicked are to lie in wait for blood: but the mouth of the upright shall deliver them.**

> *New English Bible* - The wicked are destroyed by their own words; the words of a good man are his salvation.

Proverbs 12:13 KJV - **The wicked is snared by the transgression of his lips: but the just shall come out of trouble.**

Proverbs 12:14 KJV - **A man shall be satisfied with good by the fruit of his mouth: and the recompence of a man's hands shall be rendered unto him.**

Jerusalem Bible - When a man is filled with good things, it is the fruit of his own words....

Good News Bible - Your reward depends on what you say and what you do....

Proverbs 12:18 KJV - There is that speaketh like the piercings of a sword: but the tongue of the wise is health.

Moffatt's Translation - A reckless tongue wounds like a sword, but there is healing power in thoughtful words.

Good News Bible - Thoughtless words can wound as deeply as any sword, but wisely spoken words can heal.

Basic English - There are some whose uncontrolled talk is like the wounds of a sword, but the tongue of the wise makes one well again.

Proverbs 12:25 KJV - Heaviness in the heart of man maketh it stoop: but a good word maketh it glad.

New King James - Anxiety in the heart of man causes depression; but a good word makes it glad.

Proverbs 13:3 KJV - He that keepeth his mouth keepeth his life: but he that openeth wide his lips brings destruction.

New American Bible - He who guards his mouth protects his life; to open wide one's lips brings downfall.

Good News Bible - Be careful what you say and protect your life. A careless talker destroys himself.

Moffatt's Translation - He guards his life who guards his lips....

Proverbs 16:24 KJV - Pleasant words are as an honeycomb, sweet to the soul, and health to the bones.

New American Bible - ...healthful to the body.

Proverbs 18:7 KJV - A fool's mouth is his destruction, and his lips are the snare of his soul.

Jerusalem Bible - The mouth of the fool works his own ruin, his lips are a snare for his own life.

New English Bible - The stupid man's tongue is his undoing; his lips put his life in jeopardy.

Proverbs 18:20 KJV - A man's belly shall be satisfied with the fruit of his mouth: and with the increase of his lips shall he be filled.

Good News Bible - You will have to live with the consequences of everything you say.

Proverbs 18:21 KJV - Death and life are in the power of the tongue: and they that love it shall eat the fruit thereof.

Jerusalem Bible - Death and life are in the gift of the tongue, those who indulge it must eat the fruit it yields.

Good News Bible - **What you say can preserve life or destroy it; so you must accept the consequences of your words.**

Moffatt's Translation - **Death and life are determined by the tongue....**

Proverbs 21:23 KJV - **Whoso keepeth his mouth and his tongue keepeth his soul from troubles.**

Jerusalem Bible - **He who keeps watch over his mouth and his tongue preserves himself from disaster.**

Good News Bible - **If you want to stay out of trouble, be careful what you say.**

Psychology's Great Attempt

Don't get me wrong. I'm not against psychology. Psychology is the attempt of the natural man to understand himself. Since the natural man is spiritually dead and lives totally by his soul (his mind, emotions, and personality), he cannot know his true self at all because man is a spirit. Man is not a mind or a body, he is a spirit being.

> The merely intellectual man rejects the teaching of the Spirit of God; for to him it is mere folly; he cannot grasp it.
>
> 1 Corinthians 2:14 TCNT

We must not be willing to accept anything less than what God and His Word say about us. Jesus said, "...the words that I speak unto you, they are spirit, and they are life" (John 6:63 KJV). The Greek word for spirit is *pneuma* which means "breath." God's Word carries God's breath and His Word is full of life. His Word is Him speaking to you. What He has spoken to you, must be spoken through you. You must speak and say what the Word of God says.

Pneumaspeak Labels

The Word of God is full of "pneumaspeak labels." Pneumaspeak labels describe how God sees you and who you are in Christ. Pneumaspeak labels tell you, "This is who I am, this is what I have, and this is what I can do." Begin to declare what the Word of God says you have and who you are in Christ. As you do, you will release the breath and ability of God into your life.

> ## Winning on the Inside
> IF YOU WANT WHAT GOD HAS,
> YOU MUST SAY WHAT GOD SAYS.

Pneumatherapy

Here are some "pneumaspeak labels" that come from God's Word that you should speak out of your mouth every day. This is what I call "pneumatherapy."

I Am Who God Says I Am!

- I am a child of God (Romans 8:16).

- I am redeemed from the hand of the enemy (Psalm 107:2).

- I am forgiven (Colossians 1:13,14).

- I am saved by grace through faith (Ephesians 2:8).

- I am justified (Romans 5:1).

- I am sanctified (1 Corinthians 1:30).

- I am a new creation (2 Corinthians 5:17).

- I am a partaker of His divine nature (2 Peter 1:4).

- I am redeemed from the curse of the law (Galatians 3:13).

- I am led by the Spirit of God (Romans 8:14).

- I am a son of God (Romans 8:14).

- I am delivered from the power of darkness (Colossians 1:13).

- I am kept in safety wherever I go (Psalm 91).

- I am enjoying the blessing of God (Ephesians 1:3).

- I am prospering and walking in health (3 John 2).

- I am strong in the Lord and in the power of His might (Ephesians 6:10).

- I am an heir of God and a joint heir with Jesus Christ (Romans 8:17).

- I am an heir to the blessing of Abraham (Galatians 3:14).

- I am the righteousness of God in Christ (2 Corinthians 5:21).

- I am observing and doing the commandments of the Lord (Deuteronomy 28:1).

- I am an heir of eternal life (1 John 5:11,12).

- I am healed by His stripes (1 Peter 2:24).

- I am exercising my authority over the power of the enemy (Luke 10:19).

- I am more than a conqueror (Romans 8:37).

- I am a daily overcomer of the enemy (1 John 4:4).

- I am full of peace because I am taught of the Lord (Isaiah 54:13).

- I am an overcomer by the blood of the Lamb and the word of my testimony (Revelation 12:11).

- I am not moved by what I see (2 Corinthians 4:18).

- I am walking by faith and not by sight (2 Corinthians 5:7).

- I am casting down vain and weird imaginations (2 Corinthians 10:4,5).

- I am casting all my cares upon Jesus (1 Peter 5:7).

- I am being transformed by the renewing of my mind (Romans 12:2).

- I am an imitator of Jesus (Ephesians 5:1).

- I am blessed so I can be a blessing (Genesis 12:2).

I Have What God Says I Have!

- I have been made righteous through Jesus Christ (Romans 3:21,22,24,26).

- I have been justified by the blood of Christ (Romans 5:9).

- I have been washed and sanctified by the Spirit of our God (1 Corinthians 6:11).

- I have boldness to enter into the presence of God (Hebrews 10:19; Ephesians 2:18; 3:18).

- I have peace with God through our Lord Jesus Christ (Romans 5:1).

- I have the life of God dwelling in me (John 5:24; 1 John 5:11,12).

- I have been made fit, qualified, entitled, worthy, and able to be a partaker of the inheritance of the saints in light (Colossians 1:12).

- I have been delivered from the power, authority, and dominion of darkness (Colossians 1:13).

- I have been translated into the kingdom of His dear Son (Colossians 1:13).

- I have redemption (I am redeemed and delivered) through His blood (Colossians 1:14).

- I have been forgiven through His blood (Colossians 1:14; Ephesians 1:7).

- I have been born of God (1 John 5:4).

- I have been reconciled to God (Romans 5:10).

- I have the victory through our Lord Jesus Christ (1 Corinthians 15:57).

- I have strength through our Lord (Ephesians 6:10).

- I have victory over fear (2 Timothy 1:7).

- I have power (2 Timothy 1:7).

- I have a sound mind (2 Timothy 1:7).

- I have the peace of God that surpasses all understanding (Philippians 4:7).

I Can Do What God Says I Can Do!

- I can do the works of Jesus in His name (John 14:12-14).

- I can reign in life by one, Jesus Christ (Romans 5:17).

- I can resist the devil, and he will flee from me (James 4:7).

- I can take authority over devils, in the name of Jesus (Mark 16:17; Luke 10:19).

- I can lay hands on the sick, and they shall recover (Mark 16:18).

- I can expect signs and wonders to follow me (Mark 16:17).

- I can do all things through Christ who strengthens me (Philippians 4:13).

- I can preach the gospel of our Lord Jesus Christ (Mark 16:15).

- I can go into all the world and preach the gospel (Mark 16:15; Acts 8:5-8).

- I can put on the whole armor of God (Ephesians 6:11).

- I can stand against the wiles of the devil (Ephesians 6:11).

Winning on the Inside

WHO PEOPLE SAY YOU ARE
IS NOT NEARLY AS IMPORTANT
AS WHO THE BIBLE SAYS YOU ARE.

Chapter 7

Mood Swings

I refuse to stay discouraged any longer
when I can have peace and joy.

The plans of the mind and orderly thinking belong to man, but from the Lord comes the [wise] answer of the tongue...

Roll your works upon the Lord [commit and trust them wholly to Him; He will cause your thoughts to become agreeable to His will, and] so shall your plans be established and succeed.

Proverbs 16:1,3 AMP

THE BIBLE IS A NOW BOOK, it should not only be read as a historical book. It has information from heaven in it. It's heaven's handbook for victory over your past. The Word of God has life and power in it. It is God-breathed.

All scripture is given by inspiration of God....

2 Timothy 3:16

(Swedish Translation)[5] "...given out by God... ."

(Danish Translation) [6] "...in-blown by God... ."

You cannot stay in the same situation you are in when the Word of God is being breathed in you. Transformation will begin to take place in your life because of the Word of God. That's the importance of sitting under the teaching of God's Word.

The real you is a spirit being (Proverbs 20:27; 1 Corinthians 2:11). Your spirit man needs to be fed the Word of God, which will give you power to overcome and conquer. When you get the Word of God into your spirit, it will affect your outward body as well as your spirit. It will affect your mind, your emotions, and your will. The cure for emotional problems and mood swings is to plant the Word of God on the inside of you (James 1:21). The Word will make corrections in your emotions as you meditate upon who you are and what you have in Christ.

Winning on the Inside

THE WORD OF GOD WILL MAKE CORRECTIONS IN YOUR EMOTIONS AS YOU MEDITATE UPON WHO YOU ARE AND WHAT YOU HAVE IN CHRIST.

New Creation

When some people are asked why they are having a bad day, the typical response is: "I'm going through a mid-life crisis." Or, "I am discouraged." Or, "I am codependent." Or, "I am depressed" Or, "I am a loser." Do not form a crutch for yourself with the words of your mouth. If you are speaking that, it will come into existence. Your words call your future into existence. We need to say what God's Word says. God says you are a new creation, **"Therefore, if anyone is in Christ, he is a new creation; old things have passed away, behold, all things have become new"** (2 Corinthians 5:17). I love *J. B. Phillips Translation* of this verse, **"...he becomes a new person altogether—the past is finished and gone, everything has become fresh and new."**

Days of Joy

God's Word will have an effect on your mind and emotions. Isaiah 12:3 NLT says, **"With joy you will drink deeply from the fountain of salvation!"** Verse 12 of Isaiah, chapter 55, says, **"For you shall go out with joy, and be led out with peace...."** Romans 14:17 says, **"The kingdom of God is not eating and drinking, but righteousness and peace and joy in the Holy Spirit."** One translation says, "The Kingdom of God is not coffee and donuts, but it is righteousness, peace, and joy in the Holy Ghost."

These are days of joy. Joy comes out of your spirit. It bubbles up on the inside of you, and it's contagious. Joy will spread to your mind and emotions. A sad church and sad Christians cannot win the world. Why would the world want anything that we have if we are full of sadness? Joy is medicine for your soul and heart.

Allow God's Peace to Guide You

God will always lead you with peace. You have peace in your spirit but war in your mind, because there are times your mind will try to talk you out of doing the will of God. Racing thoughts will try to distract and keep you from the peace of

God. You must let the peace of God rule your heart and your mind through Christ Jesus.

Can you imagine what was going through the minds of Peter and the other disciples when Jesus said, "Get out of the boat and walk"? They said, "You cannot do that," because it had never been done. When you do something that seems impossible, that's exactly how you do it: Obey what the Word of God and what the voice of God say rather than what your mind is saying. Your mind must be brought into agreement with the Word of God.

Verse 12 of Isaiah, chapter 55, says, **"For you shall... be led out with peace; the mountains and the hills shall break forth into singing before you...."** Your mountain will always try to breathe down the back of your neck, saying, "Impossible! Impossible! Impossible!" The mountain always says, "Impossible!" But when you are led forth with the peace of God, your mountain will begin to break forth into singing and say, "Yes, it's possible! It's possible! It's possible!" I've heard Pastor Mark Hankins say, "Don't talk to God about your mountain, talk to your mountain about your God!" Most people are talking to God about their mountain. Start talking to your mountain about your God. Tell your mountain to move!

Winning on the Inside

MOST PEOPLE ARE TALKING TO GOD ABOUT THEIR MOUNTAIN. START TALKING TO YOUR MOUNTAIN ABOUT YOUR GOD.

Fruitful Seasons Ahead

Verse 13 is the key verse I wanted to emphasize:

> Instead of the thorn shall come up the cypress tree, and instead of the brier shall come up the myrtle tree; and it shall be to the Lord for a name, for an everlasting sign that shall not be cut off.

Isaiah 55:13

I asked the Holy Spirit, "What is this thorn?" and I heard these words in my spirit: "The 'thorn' is bitterness and the pain of life." Bitterness stops people from doing the will of God. A bitter person cannot walk in God's peace, nor can they fulfill God's plan for their life.

Then I heard the Holy Spirit say, "The 'brier' is the hurt and the wounds on the inside of a person." Then He said, "Instead of bitterness, pain, and hurt, you will enter into a fruitful season." What Satan meant for evil, God will take it and turn it out for good. "[You] **shall be to the Lord for a name...**" (v. 13). One translation says, "You shall become a testimony." I heard a Baptist preacher say this once and I like it, "Satan meant it to be my tombstone, but God will take it and make it my stepping-stone."

In other words, "Instead of a thorn of bitterness, I'll make a testimony out of you. Instead of the pain of your past and the pain of your hurts and wounds, I'll make your life a testimony of My goodness and grace." Pastor Tommy Barnett said, "When life hands you a lemon, squeeze it, squeeze it good, and make yourself a glass of lemonade."

Winning on the Inside

WHAT HAS HAPPENED TO YOU IS A
SMALL THING COMPARED TO WHAT
GOD WILL DO THROUGH YOU.

Chapter 8

Heart Adjustments

I refuse to remain bound when
I am created to be free.

The law of the Lord is perfect, restoring the [whole] person....

Psalm 19:7 AMP

WE WILL FIND MANY EXAMPLES of people in the Bible who had to deal with discouragement and bitterness. Hezekiah was one of them.

The prophet Isaiah brought this word to Hezekiah:

"Set your house in order, for you shall die and not live." [That kind of a message would bring discouragement to anyone!]

Then Hezekiah turned his face toward the wall, and prayed to the Lord,

And said, "Remember now, O Lord, I pray, how I have walked before You in truth and with a loyal heart, and have done what is good in Your sight." And Hezekiah wept bitterly.

Isaiah 38:1-3

In verse 5, God spoke to Isaiah to take another message to Hezekiah: **"I have heard your prayer, I have seen your tears; surely I will add to your days fifteen years."** What Hezekiah thought was the end became a new beginning. God will do the same for you if you'll turn your face to the wall, pray, and make some heart adjustments. Before the prophet gets one block away from you, he'll have to turn around and come back with another message: "I'm going to add fifteen more years to your life. I'm going to restore your whole being."

Isaiah 38:15 shows us the type of confession Hezekiah made: **"I shall walk carefully all my years in the bitterness of my soul."** In verse 16 he said, **"O Lord, by these things men live; and in all these things is the life of my spirit; so You will restore me and make me live."**

Restored to a Better Condition

At first Hezekiah said, "I guess I'm going to have to walk all of my years in bitterness." Then he said, "No, Lord, You are going to restore me." The word *restore* means to bring back to its original condition. When God restores your life, He doesn't bring it back to where it was. He makes it better than before.

Isaiah 38:17 says:

> Indeed it was for my own peace that I had great bitterness;
> but You have lovingly delivered my soul from the pit of corrup-
> tion, for You have cast all my sins behind Your back.

Turning Things Around

I like what Hezekiah was saying: "You have lovingly delivered my soul from the pit of corruption. You took all of my
sins and cast them behind Your back." Hezekiah had severe
bitterness that was eating him up on the inside, but God
in His mercy turned things around in his life. God is in the
turning around business. It's never too late to turn your heart
toward God. Allow Him to cleanse you from all the pain and
hurt of your life. When you turn to God, the process of turning things around in your life will begin.

Winning on the Inside

WHEN YOU TURN TO GOD, THE
PROCESS OF TURNING THINGS AROUND
IN YOUR LIFE WILL BEGIN.

Sweetening the Bitter Waters

If you allow bitterness to stay in your life, it has the power
to defile you and to defile others (Hebrews 12:15). There is
an answer to bitterness. In Exodus 15, verses 24-26, the children of Israel left Egypt and crossed over the Red Sea. They
began to sing and shout on the other side of the Red Sea. They

then came to a pool of bitter water and began to drink from it. "**Now when they came to Marah, they could not drink the waters of Marah, for they were bitter...**" (Exodus 15:23). They began to murmur and to complain against Moses, "**What shall we drink?**" (v. 24).

Verse 25 says, "**So he** [Moses] **cried out to the Lord, and the Lord showed him a tree. When he cast it into the waters, the waters were made sweet....**"

The Tree of Redemption

God wants to take your pool of bitterness, your murmuring spirit, and cure it by casting the tree (cross) right in the middle of it, causing all of your bitterness to become sweet. (See Galatians 3:13; 1 Peter 2:24.) God is an expert at turning bitterness around. He can make a bitter life, a bitter heart, a bitter mind, and bitter emotions become sweet once again. He does it through the cross, through His plan of redemption. Redemption defined is "deliverance or freedom through the payment of a price." Jesus paid the price through His own blood for your freedom. The price has been PAID IN FULL! The debt is no longer in existence.

Winning on the Inside
JESUS PAID TOO HIGH OF A PRICE
FOR YOUR FREEDOM
FOR YOU TO LIVE IN BONDAGE.

I Am the Lord that Healeth Thee

The price is not only paid for your freedom from bitterness, but also for your physical healing. In Exodus 15:26 God revealed Himself to the children of Israel as their Healer.

> ...If thou wilt diligently hearken to the voice of the Lord thy God, and wilt do that which is right in his sight, and wilt give ear to his commandments, and keep all his statutes, I will put none of these diseases upon thee, which I have brought upon the Egyptians: for I am the Lord that healeth thee.
>
> Exodus 15:26 KJV

The curse of diseases was for the Egyptians—those who did not walk with God. For the believer, God reveals Himself as the Healer. Once a person makes a decision to remove bitterness from their life, they can go to the next level in receiving God's healing.

Beyond the pool of bitterness is the river of healing. In order to get into the healing river, one must cross the pool of bitterness. Bitterness is a hindrance to the healing power of God. Thank God that we have a Deliverer from bitterness.

Do you know how good it is to live free from bitterness? Without bitterness, you are sweet all the time. Bitterness comes from disappointment. God wants you to rise up over disappointment and bitterness. His Word tells us to let all bitterness be put away from you (Ephesians 4:31).

Winning on the Inside

GOD'S NOT VIEWING YOUR PAST,
HE'S FOCUSED ON YOUR FUTURE.

Chapter 9

Rising Up from the Bottom

*I refuse to stay at the bottom when
I belong at the top.*

Weeping may endure for a night, but joy comes in the morning.

Psalm 30:5 AMP

You have turned my mourning into dancing for me; You have put off my sackcloth and girded me with gladness.

Psalm 30:11 AMP

IN THE OLD TESTAMENT, David was anointed for leadership, and the Bible says he was one of God's greatest leaders. Yet he had occasion to hit the bottom because of discouragement. But the good news is, he didn't stay there. His life is an example to us of *how* to rise above discouragement and to stay on the road to recovery.

In 1 Samuel, chapter 30, David led a group of men out from the city of Ziklag to do battle. When they returned to the city, all of the men's wives and children had been taken into captivity by the enemy. Let's pick up on this story in verse 6: **"Now David was greatly distressed...."**

Have you ever been **"greatly distressed"**? There are some things in life that can cause great discouragement to come upon you. Some people think that when you are born again and filled with the Holy Spirit, you won't have any more problems. The Bible says you will have many trials, tests, and afflictions—but the Lord will deliver you out of them all (Psalm 34:19).

David wasn't just distressed. Scripture says he was **"greatly distressed."** He wasn't just having a bad day, he didn't just burn the dinner, and it wasn't just a traffic light problem—his family had been kidnapped. Jesus told us that as long as we are in the world, we will have tribulation. But He went on to say, **"Be of good cheer, I have overcome the world"** (John 16:33). *The Amplified Bible* says, **"...I have deprived it of power to harm you and have conquered it for you."**

David was so **"greatly distressed"** that Scripture says in verse 4, **"Then David and the people who were with him lifted up their voices and wept, until they had no more power to weep."** David and his men were greatly distressed, greatly discouraged.

You can hit bottom and be discouraged, but God has a plan to lift you up out of discouragement and distress and to bring you back to where you belong with Him.

Sometimes we think we're the only one on the journey when we're discouraged and distressed, but that's not the case. David is a living example of someone who was discouraged and beat down to the point where he even thought about killing himself.

When discouragement gets to the place where you want to die, dying is not the answer. God has a plan to bring you out of depression and discouragement. His plan is written down in His Word. If you will give heed and obey His Word, He will bring you out.

Winning on the Inside

DON'T POISON YOUR FUTURE BY
BEING CONTROLLED BY YOUR PAST.

Discouragement—A Tool of Satan

Sometimes people get discouraged and depressed to the point where it seems like their life is not valuable anymore. That's when we begin to listen to the devil who will get right up in your ear. If the devil can get you to listen to him, it won't be long that he will try to get control of your thought life. I believe God has some supernatural, Holy Ghost Q-tips to get the devil out of your ear!

Sometimes we foolishly talk as if the devil has all the power, but the only stronghold he has in our lives comes through openings such as fear, worry, and ignorance of God's Word. If we allow the devil to remain in our thought life, he will begin to control our life. His plan is to bring you down, to bring you to the bottom. He wants you to believe the lie that you are no good and not loved. It's a downward spiral. He wants you to begin to look at your circumstances. He wants you to focus in on how you are mistreated. He wants you to see how bad things are so he can bring discouragement. Why?

- Discouraged people do not have power over their past.

- Discouraged people cannot be a witness of joy and victory.

- Discouraged people are always focused on themselves rather than on the harvest of souls.

- Discouraged people don't believe the truth applies to them.

This is why the devil wants the Church to be discouraged and in financial lack. He wants the Church to focus on their circumstances rather than on the lost souls who are waiting to be brought into God's Kingdom.

Discouragement steals the dream out of your heart. For anyone who is a dreamer, there will always be a schemer. And that schemer is the devil. His schemes are to rob you and kill the God-given dream that is in your heart.

Sometimes we think that a certain person is our problem. But people are not your problem. The enemy is behind every person who does evil and harm to you. The Bible says, **"We do not wrestle against flesh and blood..."** (Ephesians 6:12).

> For we are not fighting against people made of flesh and blood, but against persons without bodies—the evil rulers of the unseen world....
>
> Ephesians 6:12 TLB

Our battle is a spiritual battle, and the enemy wants to deceive you so he can get you off course. If he can get you to believe a lie, then he can get you off course.

God has a good plan for you in His Word. It was established before you were ever born. His plan was laid out for your life before your parents ever thought of you, and before your grandparents ever thought of your parents.

God's plan for you is good. You don't have to worry whether God is going to take you to the edge and destroy you or whip something on you. God is a good God, and we are New Covenant creatures. Many people are living under the Old Covenant. They have been Old Covenant taught, but we're living under a New Covenant of grace and mercy.

David Encouraged Himself in the Lord

First Samuel 30:6 says:

> Now David was greatly distressed, for the people spoke of stoning him, because the soul of all the people was grieved, every man for his sons and his daughters. But David strengthened himself in the Lord his God.

The King James Version of this verse says, **"David encouraged himself in the Lord his God."**

There's a way to turn your stress to encouragement. It's not all up to God. Sometimes we sit back and say, "I'm waiting on God to do it. When is God going to move?" Or, "I'm waiting on the prophet to come by." Or, "I'm waiting on a miracle." We're not waiting on God. He has already moved. In His death, burial, and resurrection, God already did everything for you and me that He is ever going to do.

Because of Jesus' triumph at Calvary, you are already delivered. In redemption, it's sealed. It belongs to you. Your victory has already been deposited in your account. You are already free.

David sought God's plan of deliverance:

> So David inquired of the Lord, saying, "Shall I pursue this troop? Shall I overtake them?" And He answered him, "Pursue, for you shall surely overtake them and without fail recover all."
>
> 1 Samuel 30:8

David had a conversation going with God. You can talk to God and God will talk to you. He wants you to communicate with Him. You don't have to put on a religious face when you talk to God. You don't have to say, "Oh, God, who created the universe." He knows that's not you!

Can you imagine a Cajun[7] trying to talk that way? No, a Cajun is going to talk in Cajun to God, and God can understand him. When we think about talking to God, sometimes we think we have to act like someone else. Just be yourself!

I like what Peter did when he began to sink. He cried out to the Lord. He didn't have time to say: "Oh, Jesus of Nazareth, who traveled through Capernaum; who turned the water into wine; who performs miracles; who descended down from heaven; who was born of a virgin; who was deity in the flesh; who was predestined to die on the cross; whose body was put in the tomb and three days later raised from the dead." You don't have time to say all of that when you are knee-deep. Peter would have drowned by the time he prayed that prayer!

Some people believe we have to pray long and loud to get God's attention. I know I'm kicking over some sacred cows.

When you are sinking, or you're going down, just cry out to the Lord like Peter did: "Lord, save me!"

I was teaching about Peter walking on the water at a Church of God in Christ in Arkansas, at an anniversary celebration for a pastor. After I finished preaching, another minister came to the pulpit. It was tag team night. He said, "What I like about that sermon is how Peter prayed." He said, "Peter had short prayers for high waves!" I like that: Short prayers for high waves!

God is a delivering God. He promised in His Word to deliver you, to never forget you, and to never leave you nor forsake you. He said, "I'll be with you to the end." But if we listen to our mind, we think we're the only one who has a problem. "Nobody in the world is going through what I'm going through right now. I'm the only one."

I have news for you. Many people have gone through it, and they have come out on the other side.

Isaiah 43:1,2 is a powerful promise of deliverance for you and me:

> "Fear not, for I have redeemed you; I have called you by your name; you are Mine.
>
> "When you pass through the waters, I will be with you; and through the rivers, they shall not overflow you. When you walk through the fire, you shall not be burned, nor shall the flame scorch you."

Pray the Answer

Pray the answer, not the problem. The answer is in God's Word. The Bible says, "...I am alert and active, watching over My word to perform it" (Jeremiah 1:12 AMP).

Commit yourself to pray these prayers daily.

That the God of our Lord Jesus Christ, the Father of glory, may give to you (me) the spirit of wisdom and revelation in the knowledge of Him, the eyes of your (my) understanding being enlightened; that you (I) may know what is the hope of His calling, what are the riches of the glory of His inheritance in the saints, and what is the exceeding greatness of his power toward us who believe, according to the working of His mighty power which He worked in Christ when He raised Him from the dead and seated Him at His right hand in the heavenly places, far above all principality and power and might and dominion, and every name that is named, not only in this age but also in that which is to come. And He put all things under His feet, and gave Him to be head over all things to the church, which is His body, the fullness of Him who fills all in all.

Ephesians 1:17-23

For this reason I bow my knees to the Father of our Lord Jesus Christ, from whom the whole family in heaven and earth is named, that He would grant you, according to the riches of His glory, to be strengthened with might through His Spirit in the inner man, that Christ may dwell in your hearts through faith; that you, being rooted and grounded in love, may be able to comprehend with all the saints what is the width and length and depth and height—to know the love of Christ which passes knowledge; that you may be filled with all the fullness of God. Now to Him who is able to do exceedingly abundantly above all that we ask or think, according to the power that works in us, to Him be glory in the church by Christ Jesus to all generations, forever and ever. Amen.

Ephesians 3:14-21

Winning on the Inside

SETBACKS ARE OPPORTUNITIES FOR
GOD TO MOVE IN YOUR LIFE.

Deliverance in Fiery Trials

We have many promises and examples in God's Word of deliverance from fiery trials. How about Shadrach, Meshach, and Abednego? When you get in the fiery furnace, that's when the Fourth Man shows up! (See Daniel 3:10-30.)

When you are in a test or a trial, or you're in trouble, or when you miss it, God won't leave you. The Word of God says, "…I am with you always, even unto the end of the age" (Matthew 28:20).

Not only do we have promises in the Word for ourselves, but there are promises for our children, too. Sometimes even grown children make mistakes. It hurts a parent's heart to see their children make mistakes. But when they do mess up and get in the fiery furnace, God says, "I will not leave them." The Fourth Man will show up and deliver our children, too.

The thing I like about Shadrach, Meshach, and Abednego is that they were thrown bound into the fiery furnace. It wasn't long until King Nebuchadnezzar said, **"Did we not cast three men bound into the midst of the fire?...Look!...I see four men loose, walking in the midst of the fire; and they are not hurt, and the form of the fourth is like the Son of God"** (Daniel 3:24,25).

Can you imagine being loosed in the middle of your trial? Can you imagine being free? Can you imagine counting it all joy? The Bible says, **"Count it all joy when you fall into various trials"** (James 1:2). Is it possible to have joy in the midst of a trial? Is it possible that God can turn your discouragement to joy and peace?

Can you imagine Shadrach, Meshach, and Abednego walking around in the fiery furnace loosed, with flames coming up on all sides of them, and suddenly the king looks in and sees a fourth person who looks like the Son of God? I tell you, we have the Fourth Man in the fiery furnace with us right now. You don't have to have a word from a prophet to know that God is a delivering God. The Fourth Man still shows up in the fiery furnace of trials.

There are two sides of God. Most people focus on the ability of God, but there is the willingness of God to consider, too. God is able to deliver you, and He is also willing to deliver you.

Winning on the Inside

GOD IS NOT ONLY ABLE
TO DELIVER YOU, HE IS ALSO WILLING
TO DELIVER YOU!

David asked, **"Shall I pursue?"** The Lord said, **"Pursue, for you shall surely overtake them and without fail RECOVER all"** (1 Samuel 30:8).

Like David, you're not going to fail. One of the biggest things that stops people from doing anything is the fear of failure. God said, **"You shall...without fail recover all"** (v. 8). God didn't say David would recover 35, 55, 65, or 75 percent. He said, "I'm going to bump you up to *all.* You are going to recover *all.*"

In Nahum 1:9 there is a wonderful promise to claim, which says, **"He will make an utter end of it** [your bondage]. **Affliction will not rise up a second time."** Remember, **"Joy comes in the morning!"**

Winning on the Inside

MY PAST IS ONLY AS PAINFUL AS I
ALLOW IT TO BE.

— 105 —

Chapter 10

"Down" Is a Dirty, Four-Letter Word

*I refuse to speak words of defeat when
I can speak words of freedom.*

But none of these things move me, neither count I my life dear unto myself, so that I might finish my course with joy, and the ministry, which I have received of the Lord Jesus, to testify the gospel of the grace of God.

Acts 20:24 KJV

IN THE NEW TESTAMENT, we learn about a remarkable apostle, Paul—a man who would not quit. One of the greatest characteristics of your life should be, "I will not quit." Regardless of what the devil does, if you won't quit, you will beat him. If you quit, that's when you are defeated.

Some people are counting the score. We're not counting the score. We're just counting how many times you get back up! If you keep getting back up, you are going to win.

In 2 Corinthians 4:8, Paul said, **"We are hard-pressed on every side...."** To be hard-pressed means to be tried to the point that you want to give up or quit. What is Satan after when we get in a fiery trial? He's not after us; he's after our faith. It's called "the trial of your faith."

Faith pleases God (Hebrews 11:6). Faith moves mountains. Faith takes you out of the natural walk and puts you into the supernatural arena where God walks. That's why Satan wants to stop your faith, because faith will give you a supernatural run at life.

Winning on the Inside

FAITH WILL GIVE YOU A
SUPERNATURAL RUN AT LIFE.

Faith isn't just a shout. It's a walk. It's a walk and a shout! Scripture says, **"The just shall live by faith"** (Hebrews 10:38). In order to live by faith, you have to keep your faith strong. There are enemies of your faith, and they are advancing and attacking. When people are hard-pressed, sometimes they begin to look at their circumstances.

> We are hard-pressed on every side, yet not crushed; we are perplexed, but not in despair;
>
> Persecuted, but not forsaken; struck down, but not destroyed.
>
> 2 Corinthians 4:8,9

Some people focus on being hard-pressed or troubled, but we need to focus in on "not destroyed"!

Most people aren't focused on your failures. Sometimes we think we're disqualified because we've missed the mark, and everybody knows we've missed the mark. Most people aren't thinking about your missing the mark. They're thinking about their own life. But the devil will tell you, "Everybody in the church is thinking about you, because you've missed the mark." That's a lie!

The truth is, people aren't trying to keep you down. Most people would be encouraged to see you rise up and do the will of God, because they realize they have missed it at times, too.

As long as there is air in your lungs, you have the ability to rise up and do what God has called you to do. As long as there is faith in your heart, you can still rise up and do what God has called you to do. It's not how many times you've been knocked down, or how many times you've missed the mark, but can you get back up? God is waiting on you to get back up.

Encouraging Yourself

"David encouraged himself in the Lord his God" (1 Samuel 30:6 KJV). So what does encouragement mean? It means "to urge others or yourself to hold fast to the principles of faith." There are times you need to have a conversation with yourself, look yourself in the mirror and say, "You in the mirror, you've got to hold fast to the principles of faith!"

Encouragement means "to affirm (validate or uphold); to inspire with courage, spirit, or hope."[8] Husbands and wives are looking for affirmation from each other. For example, when I mow the yard and ask my wife, "Honey, how does the yard look?" I want her approval. Or perhaps the husband walks into the house and his wife has cleaned the carpet and rearranged the furniture. She asks, "How does it look?" She, too, is looking for affirmation or approval.

Affirmation won't always come from people. Sometimes you may need to affirm yourself, just as David did. He encouraged himself in the Lord. "Man, you're doing good! I can rise up, because I can do all things through Christ who strengthens me."

You can encourage yourself by saying: "You're full of the faith of God! You have faith to overcome the world, and you're going to walk in love and victory today. You're going to be a blessing to others."

Winning on the Inside
A BEAUTIFUL LIFE IS ONE THAT
ALLOWS GOD TO RESTORE.

Revival in a Small Town

The first time I really remember hearing any teaching on faith and the baptism in the Holy Spirit was in January of 1976. It was a big encouragement to me. I remember the morning well. My mother woke me up for Sunday school and said, "Get up and get ready for church because the former quarterback for the football team is going to be speaking." Growing up in the small town of Magnolia, Arkansas, I attended a church called Bethel Full Gospel Church. Although our church had only about seventy-five members in those days, God had great plans for that place and for those people.

I had already surrendered my life to be a preacher at a young age of twelve—the year after God touched me at the Kathryn Kuhlman crusade in Tulsa. I had an encounter with God, but I didn't truly know that the Holy Spirit was for me. I thought that you had to tarry to receive Him. I knew I experienced His presence once or twice at youth camp, but His presence often seemed to fade after I got home.

That Sunday morning appeared to be just like every other Sunday. I didn't see too many new people. I was sitting up front on the second row of the church between two of my friends, Butch and Becky. After the song service, Pastor Henry Pletcher introduced the evangelist who would be with us for two weeks. I said to myself, "Two weeks, you've got to be kidding me. We can't go to church for two weeks."

The Spirit of Faith

Then the evangelist took the microphone and began to speak. To be totally honest, I wasn't too impressed with the man or with his wife. The evangelist said something funny and his wife began to laugh. She laughed real low and then, he began to laugh at a high pitch. The congregation chuckled. I thought to myself that God had made a mistake, because when the evangelist's wife laughed she seemed to have his laugh and he seemed to have hers. (It was funny!)

The evangelist who I thought was messing up my schedule was Billy Joe Daugherty and his wife, Sharon. His teaching was simple and full of faith. There was something about hearing faith that made my spirit leap within. The meetings went on and revival began to hit our church. People were coming from all over to hear this young evangelist. At this time I was even giving my endorsement to the meetings. Our city was talking about our church and the outpouring of God's Spirit. Every night Billy Joe and Sharon were praying for the sick and leading people in the baptism of the Holy Spirit and laughter. The Spirit of faith was upon them to carry our church to a new level.

> We having the same spirit of faith, according as it is written, I believed, and therefore have I spoken; we also believe, and therefore speak.
>
> 2 Corinthians 4:13 KJV

Winning on the Inside

THE SPIRIT OF FAITH WILL ALWAYS
CARRY YOU TO NEW LEVELS.

This was my first taste of revival and the teaching of faith, which now has become a way of life for me. One night most of the youth got filled with the Holy Spirit and something began to burn in my heart for more of the things of God. I was no longer satisfied with what I had, and I was not willing to stay where I was any longer. Our church was on fire and more than a thousand visitors came to be a part of the revival that lasted for six weeks at our little Full Gospel church.

Turning Point

During that meeting Billy Joe laid hands on me several times. It wasn't long until our meeting came to an end, but the fire was still burning within the hearts of the people. Many pastors I know today were called to preach during that meeting. They say that the revival of 1976 at Bethel was the turning point in their lives. As a sixteen-year-old, I received the encouragement that I needed to keep my life on course.

Faith, Courage, and Boldness

Living the life of faith requires not only encouragement, but also courage and boldness. The book of Joshua has a lot to say about courage. Webster defines courage as "mental or moral strength to venture, persevere, and withstand dangers, fear, or difficulty."[9] Chapter 1, verse 6, says, **"Be strong and of good courage...."** The Lord would not have told Joshua to be strong if he didn't have the ability within himself to be strong. It's a choice to be strong. Sometimes we think it's a "feeling," but it's not. Your feelings can deceive you. You can be strong in faith by confessing and declaring what the Word of God says.

When your feelings are trying to lead you astray is the time to make the most Word declarations. When we're at our lowest, we ought to stand up and say, "I'm going to declare the Word of the Lord." At that point, I believe that there is more power released because we are being strong in the Lord. The choice is ours. We can be as strong in the Lord as we want to be, or we can be weak. That may shock you, but you can be strong today. If you are a weak Christian, it's because of your own choice, for there is power available to us in God's Word.

God said to Joshua:

> Be strong and of good courage, for to this people you shall divide as an inheritance the land which I swore to their fathers to give them.

> Only be strong and very courageous, that you may observe to do according to all the law which Moses My servant commanded you; do not turn from it to the right hand or to the left....

Joshua 1:6,7

In other words, don't waver. When you're walking on the water is the wrong time to take your eyes off of Jesus. Don't look to the right or to the left. Don't get distracted. Don't compromise. Don't look to the world. Don't look to sin. Don't look to what your neighbors are enjoying.

> Only be strong and very courageous...that you may prosper wherever you go...

> Have I not commanded you? Be strong and of good courage; do not be afraid [He's dealing with fear], nor be dismayed [or discouraged], for the Lord your God is with you wherever you go.

Joshua 1:7,9

Have you ever been in a situation where fear has tried to creep into your mind? God is saying, "Don't allow fear to master you or control you." You may be asking, "What do you mean to not *allow* fear?" God has given you power over fear.

When fear begins to speak to you, you've got to speak back to it: "No, you don't, fear, in Jesus' name. God has not given me a spirit of fear, but He has given me power, love, and a sound mind" (2 Timothy 1:7).

You need a sound mind, because that's where the battle takes place—not in your heart or in your body, but in your mind. *The Amplified Translation* of 2 Timothy 1:7 says God has given us a **"calm and well-balanced mind and discipline and self-control."** The devil wants to get in your mind. That's why we have to renew our mind with the Word of God. By believing and speaking the promises of God's Word, you can keep fearful thoughts out and allow the peace of God to rule in your mind.

Winning on the Inside

FEAR WILL FREEZE YOU AND HOLD YOU IN BONDAGE, FAITH WILL ALLOW YOU TO BREAK BARRIERS.

Get Bold with the Devil!

When the devil sends a thought that's not in line with God's Word, kick it out, in Jesus' name. The Bible teaches you to cast down or throw wrong thoughts out of your mind (2 Corinthians 10:5). You've got to get forceful and bold with the devil.

Recently, we opened up the doors to our house to let fresh air in because the weather was so cool and beautiful. What would you do if you were airing out your house, leaving the front doors open, and while you're in the back of your house an old pig, stinky and filthy, dripping with slop, walks up your driveway and walks into your house? He comes right in from the pigpen and sits in your favorite chair. You are busy in the back room, so you don't even know the pig has come in your house.

You walk into the living room and the pig is now stretched out on your couch! What would you do? You wouldn't say, "Now, isn't that sweet?" Yet that's how a lot of people are with the devil. They don't get bold. They don't take authority over the devil, because they always want someone else to deal with the devil for them.

You wouldn't call someone and say, "Come over here and get this pig out of my house." Or, "Isn't that a pretty pig?" Or, "That's Miss Piggy." Or, "That's Arnold. Isn't he cute?" I mean, you would go and get a 2 x 4, or a gun. You'd get violent and get the pig out of your house, or you would have pork chops for dinner.

Too many times we have let the devil come right in and we say, "Now, come off that couch, you little thing, you." You've got to take authority over the devil. That authority has been given to you in Jesus' name. **"Behold, I give you the authority to trample on serpents and scorpions, and over all the power of the enemy, and nothing shall by any means hurt you"** (Luke 10:19).

There comes a time when you've got to be bold and strong and full of courage. You can't allow fear to conquer your life. Stand up and say, "God hasn't given me a spirit of fear. I'm not allowing these pigs to stay in my mind, because if I have pig thoughts and pig slop in my mind, eventually I will have pig speaking and pig living!" Remember, you can finish your course with joy!

Winning on the Inside

HOLDING ON, SOMETIMES, IS NOT AS
IMPORTANT AS LETTING GO.

Chapter 11

Seven Steps to Winning on the Inside

I refuse to lose when I know that I can win.

> But thanks be to God, Who in Christ always leads us in triumph [as trophies of Christ's victory] and through us spreads and makes evident the fragrance of the knowledge of God everywhere.
>
> 2 Corinthians 2:14 AMP

HERE ARE SEVEN STEPS TO WINNING ON THE INSIDE:

1. *Stay in the right environment.* To win within, you must be in the right environment. The environment I am speaking about is an environment of prayer.

If you study the life of Jesus, you'll find that He spent a lot of His time in prayer, and He didn't have three or four prayer partners. In fact, you'll find that Jesus prayed alone much of the time. The Bible says that Jesus got up early in the morning to pray. Then He prayed throughout the day. Sometimes He spent the entire night in prayer. At times He went to the mountains or to the wilderness to pray where He could be alone to commune with His Father.

If the Son of God had to pray, surely you and I need to pray. If your prayer life goes down, it won't be long until discouragement will try to land on your life. When we stay prayed up, the devil cannot affect us.

The Bible says, **"Pray without ceasing"** (1 Thessalonians 5:17). You can pray while you're driving, and you can even pray in the Spirit while you are on your job. But nothing will ever replace time alone or time away with the Father.

Winning on the Inside
NOTHING WILL EVER REPLACE
TIME ALONE WITH YOUR
HEAVENLY FATHER.

Jesus said, **"But you, when you pray, go into your room, and when you have shut your door, pray to your Father who is in the secret place; and your Father who sees in secret will reward you openly"** (Matthew 6:6). The reason we don't have what we need is because we haven't spent enough time in the right environment—in our prayer closet.

2. Stay edified. First Corinthians 14:4 says, **"He who speaks in a tongue edifies himself, but he who prophesies edifies the church."** When you pray in the Holy Ghost, you edify yourself.

Jude 20,21 says:

> But you, beloved, building yourselves up on your most holy faith, praying in the Holy Spirit, keep yourselves in the love of God....

There is a connection between praying in the Spirit and walking in love, so keep yourself edified.

3. *Eliminate distractions.* To win within one must eliminate all distractions. In earlier days, blinders were used to prevent mules from being distracted by other mule teams to their right or to their left. The blinders kept them looking straight ahead, doing their own job.

We need some spiritual blinders so we won't be distracted. Mark 4:19 tells us of three things that are designed to distract us: **"The cares of this world, the deceitfulness of riches, and the desires for other things...."** These distractions, according to Mark, enter in to **"choke the word, and it** [the Word] **becomes unfruitful."**

This verse in *The Amplified Translation* says:

> The cares and anxieties of the world and DISTRACTIONS of the age, and the pleasure and delight and false glamour and deceitfulness of riches, and the craving and passionate desire for other things creep in and choke and suffocate the Word, and it becomes fruitless.

Eliminate whatever is distracting you. Put your blinders on and keep your focus on Jesus.

4. *Enhance yourself in the Lord.* To enhance means to become greater, mightier, to see yourself as a person of value, to become God-inside-minded, knowing that the God who created the world lives on the inside of you.

Winning on the Inside

YOU MUST SEE YOURSELF THE
WAY GOD CREATED YOU,
A PERSON OF VALUE.

First John 4:4 says, "**He who is in you** [Jesus] **is greater than he** [the devil] **who is in the world.**" This is one of the Scriptures that I was taught as a little boy in my small, Full Gospel church. The One in you is greater than what you are facing in the world.

John 16:33 says, "**In the world you will have tribulation; but be of good cheer, I have overcome the world.**" All the outward tribulation in the world cannot stop you from winning on the inside! You are already a winner in Christ.

5. *Become established in "who you are in Christ."*

In the first few verses of Ephesians, chapter 1, Paul says:

- God has blessed *you* with every spiritual blessing.

- God has chosen *you*.

- God has adopted *you*.

- God has made *you* accepted in the Beloved.

- God has redeemed *you* through Jesus Christ, His Son.

- God has forgiven *you*.

- God causes His grace to abound toward *you*.

- God has made known to *you* the mystery of His will.

- In Jesus Christ *you* have obtained an inheritance.

There is no way you can go under and be defeated if all you know is, "I am blessed and I am chosen of God." The devil looks so small compared to the Bible when you realize you are blessed, chosen, and adopted. To be adopted has special meaning. When you are born into a family, you are automatically accepted, but when you are adopted, that means someone made a decision to accept you, not by force, but by choice, out of love.

6. *Evaluate your relationships.*

In relationships there are two words which come to mind that we need to discuss: "no" and "boundaries."

To be a winner on the inside you have to know when to say "no." No is not a bad word, it could mean, "not now," "enough," "I don't have time," or it could simply mean "no." Winners know when to say "no," and they know when to say "yes." Yes is not always the answer. Sometimes yes means "more responsibility," "more time," and "more sacrifice."

True relationships are always a two-way road, not a one-way, my way lane. Unhealthy relationships are one way. This is where the word "boundaries" comes in. Healthy boundaries are necessary until trust is built within your life.

Winning on the Inside

HEALTHY BOUNDARIES ARE
NECESSARY UNTIL TRUST IS BUILT
WITHIN YOUR LIFE.

Boundaries are healthy for everyone. Here are some boundaries that you need to be aware of: "Everyone needs time alone," "Everyone needs time off," and "Everyone needs time away from the action." I'm not talking about a year off; I'm talking about a few days or weeks away to pray and rest. You might as well face it, Holy Joe, rest is of God!

We live in a go-go world, and sometimes the best answer is to simply say "NO."

7. *Live in expectation.* To remain encouraged, you must live in expectation.

Jeremiah 29:11 says:

> For I know the thoughts that I think toward you, says the Lord, thoughts of peace and not of evil, to give you a future and a hope [or an expectation].

The New International Version says:

> "For I know the plans I have for you," declares the Lord, "plans to prosper you and not to harm you, plans to give you hope and a future."

When your expectation is in God, it won't be cut off. It will come to pass. I have learned to live in expectation. Oral Roberts said, "Expect a miracle!" You can't get a miracle if you're not expecting one.

Proverbs 23:18 AMP says:

> For surely there is a latter end [a future and a reward], and your hope and expectation shall not be cut off.

I've got news for you. Discouragement can't keep you down. You're going over. You're not going to fail. You are going to recover all and win! In the final chapter, you will discover how to apply the winning touch that puts bitterness and pain away from you, forever!

Chapter 12

Applying the Cure!

I refuse to remain sick when I can recover.

The Lord is my Shepherd [to feed, guide, and shield me], I shall not lack...

He refreshes and restores my life (my self)....

Psalm 23:1,3 AMP

WELCOME TO THE "RECOVERY ZONE." Throughout this book, we have talked about "winning on the inside" and "the road to recovery" from the pain of the past. Now, let's summarize these solutions and begin to apply them to our lives.

Path to Wholeness

Cure #1—One of the cures for bitterness is *fellowship with God and His family*. This is your "path to wholeness."

Often, a person with bitterness tends to avoid people because they are full of hurt, pain, and mistrust. Because they have been rejected and betrayed, they try to avoid communicating and fellowshipping with others.

God did not call you to be an island to yourself. He has called you to be part of His family, a part of the Body of Christ. When all of the parts of the Body come together, it gives increase and it supplies the entire Body. God didn't call you to be fed only by Christian TV or tapes. He called you to a Body, to a local church, and to a pastor.

> God is faithful, by whom you were called into the fellowship of His Son, Jesus Christ our Lord.
>
> 1 Corinthians 1:9

You can get on a new path today—the path to wholeness—by making a decision to fellowship with God and with other believers. Today we are living in the age of support groups; everybody is going to "group."

My suggestion for you is to get plugged into your local church. Join the true support group—the Mountain Mover Support Group. Don't live another day in fear of people or what people think. I heard Dr. Lester Sumrall say, "In someone else's mind is a sad place to keep your joy."

Winning on the Inside

THE PATH TO WHOLENESS IS
THROUGH FELLOWSHIP WITH GOD.

Path to Healing

Cure #2—Another cure for bitterness is *the love of God.* This is your "path to healing" from all the anger, bitterness, resentment, and pain you've carried.

You can get on the path to healing today by acknowledging and accepting God's love for you. In Romans 5:5 the scripture states, **"The love of God has been poured out in our hearts by the Holy Spirit who was given to us."** This divine love is abiding within those who are born of the Spirit. This love is above offense and bitterness. Once you allow this love to master your inner life, your victory is at hand.

As you read *The Amplified Version* of 1 Corinthians 13:4-8, you will discover the depth of God's love that abides within the believer (Ephesians 3:16-20). One must allow this love to grow within and make this love walk their ultimate goal in life.

The person who chooses to walk in love chooses God's best for their life and refuses to allow the past to control and conquer them.

Love endures long and is patient and kind; love never is envious nor boils over with jealousy, is not boastful or vainglorious, does not display itself haughtily.

It is not conceited (arrogant and inflated with pride); it is not rude (unmannerly) and does not act unbecomingly. Love (God's love in us) does not insist on its own rights or its own way, for it is not self-seeking; it is not touchy or fretful or resentful; it takes no account of the evil done to it [it pays no attention to a suffered wrong].

It does not rejoice at injustice and unrighteousness, but rejoices when right and truth prevail.

Love bears up under anything and everything that comes, is ever ready to believe the best of every person, its hopes are fadeless under all circumstances, and it endures everything [without weakening].

Love never fails [never fades out or becomes obsolete or comes to an end]....

1 Corinthians 13:4-8 AMP

My suggestion to you is to take these verses from 1 Corinthians, chapter 13, and quote them four times a day. Allow these verses to penetrate your life. Once you make this scripture a way of life, nothing can control you and stop you.

Winning on the Inside
THE PATH TO HEALING IS THROUGH THE LOVE OF GOD.

Path to Completeness

Cure #3—Another cure for bitterness is *forgiveness*. This is your "path to completeness." As I mentioned earlier, to release and forgive a person is really a gift to yourself. It is the primary key to your liberty from bitterness. Forgiveness brings closure to the pain of the past and the beginning of a new day. You will never be a true winner with unforgiveness in your life. You always win when you walk in love and forgiveness.

Forgiveness takes faith. Your emotions will try to fight you and to keep you in anger, but they will change. Your feelings will follow your faith. Faith is an act. You have to walk out your forgiveness every day. Your feelings will line up with your faith in time. It may take days or months, but your feelings will get in line with your acts of love.

> And whenever you stand praying, if you have anything against anyone, forgive him [or her], that your Father in heaven may also forgive you your trespasses.

Mark 11:25

My suggestion to you is to do what Jesus told you to do in Matthew 5:44: **"Love your enemies, bless those who curse you, do good to those who hate you, and pray for those who spitefully use you and persecute you."** Let's try it: love, bless, do good, and pray. Cleansing will take place in your heart when you walk in love toward the one who hurt you, then follow up with blessing them in the name of Jesus Christ. Refuse to say anything bad about the person who hurt you. In fact, say something good. Then pray your best prayer over that person.

Winning on the Inside
THE PATH TO COMPLETENESS IS THROUGH FORGIVENESS.

Path to Acceptance

Cure #4 - Another cure for bitterness is *the blood of Jesus*, which is your "path to acceptance." The blood of Jesus will wash and cleanse you once you relinquish all rights to hold and nurse your hurts. You are accepted in the Beloved (Ephesians 1:6), and you will realize that you have the power to accept others. You'll begin to open up to other people and your relationships will become stronger and healthier. You will lose the fear of getting too close to others, and rejections will be dealt with in your life. Once you receive God's love on the basis of His righteousness, you can freely accept and love others.

Step into the path of acceptance today by allowing the blood of Jesus to wash and cleanse you.

> But if we walk in the light as He is in the light, we have fellowship with one another, and the blood of Jesus Christ His Son cleanses us from all sin.
>
> 1 John 1:7
>
> To Him who loved us and washed us from our sins in His own blood.
>
> Revelation 1:5
>
> [With] His own blood, having found and secured a complete redemption (an everlasting release for us).
>
> Hebrews 9:12 AMP

In Kirbyjon H. Caldwell's book, *The Gospel of Good Success*,[10] he describes three simple parameters to a God-blessed relationship. As I read them they blessed my life and I wanted to share them with you.

1. The relationship meets your need.

2. The relationship is growing.

3. The relationship doesn't require your constantly asking God for forgiveness.

My suggestion to you is to set new priorities for your life, starting with God. Get to know Him (Philippians 3:10 AMP) before you get to know anybody else. Strong fellowship with your Heavenly Father will create healthy relationships with others.

Winning on the Inside

THE PATH TO ACCEPTANCE IS
THROUGH THE BLOOD OF CHRIST.

Path to Change

Cure #5—Another cure for bitterness and pain is *the glory of God*—the presence of God—which is your "path to change." Pastor Mark Hankins always says, "It takes changes to get into the glory, and it takes the glory to make changes." If you want to get in the glory where there is healing, it will take changes on your part. But once you get into the glory, it will bring changes into your life.

> But we all...beholding...the glory of the Lord, are being transformed into the same image from glory to glory....
>
> 2 Corinthians 3:18

No longer do you have to be one of the walking wounded or a victim. You are on the path of wholeness, healing, completeness, acceptance–the path that brings change. You may have damaged feelings and emotions, but healing comes in the glory. You are not a reject; that's a lie of the devil.

I've heard people say, "I can never love anyone again." You can be loved, and you can love again because your emotions are not damaged anymore. Your feelings are subject to the glory. The Great Physician is in, and He makes house calls twenty-four hours a day!

God has the medication and the vitamins you need in His Word to change any situation, but His Word must be given first place in your life.

You may have been in a mental ward or a stress unit time and time again. The words of your psychiatrist and/or psychologist and counselors have helped you reason why you are what you are (naturally speaking); cope with pressures and discover ways to resolve anger, and many other useful tools. Basically, they deal with your soul (mind, will, and emotions). Many of these principles are based on the Word of God. However, some may fall short of bringing hope of a real cure. Only knowing spiritual truths and applying these truths will bring freedom. **"You shall know the truth, and the truth shall make you free"** (John 8:32). Jesus is the Truth! He ministers hope, peace, and direction. **He is the Living Bread**. (John 6:51.)

Pneumatrist

The Holy Spirit is your Counselor, Strengthener, and Comforter (read John 14:16 AMP). "Spirit" in the Greek is *pneuma*. That's why I call the Holy Spirit my "Pneumatrist," because He speaks Spirit to spirit. He is speaking "Spirit" words to your heart now.

You are a spirit (read 1 Thessalonians 5:23; Job 32:8) and the Holy Spirit will strengthen the real you (read Ephesians 3:16) and keep your inner man strong. The power of your Creator and the Father of spirits is not only in His Word, but this power lives in you! A strong spirit will have a positive effect on your mind and emotions. A strong spirit will cause everything that is out of order to get back in line with God's plan.

> And what is the exceeding greatness of His power toward us [in us] who believe, according to the working of His mighty power.

> Ephesians 1:19

> Now to Him who is able to do exceedingly abundantly above all that we ask or think, according to the power that works in us.

> Ephesians 3:20

Pneumatherapy

Pneumatherapy is Spirit to spirit communication. It is agreeing with the Spirit of Truth, saying what He says, rather than what you think about yourself. Believing His thoughts toward you are greater than your thoughts, knowing they will bring great change. We activate the power of the Word by speaking. Say this now: "I am not my own, I have been purchased with a great price, the precious blood of Jesus Christ." You belong to Him. Pneumatherapy is saying what God says about you. Say this with me: "I have died, and now my life is hid with Christ in God." (1 Corinthians 6:19-20, 1 Peter 1:19.) Trust the Greater One, He will hold you, carry you, lift you out of your present circumstance. **"...because the one who is in you is greater than the one who is in the world"** (1 John 4:4 NIV). There is nothing, no power in this present life which can deny you from knowing His glory. The Holy Spirit overcomes all negative thoughts and emotions. The power of His presence brings peace, joy, and freedom. It doesn't matter how desperate your situation may be. The spirit of glory is in you to bring you out. "But as for me, I watch in hope for the Lord, I wait for God my Savior; my God will hear me. Do not gloat over me, my enemy! Though I have fallen, I will rise. Though I sit in darkness, the Lord will be my light... He will bring me out into the light; I will see his righteousness" (Micah 7:7-9 NIV).

Decision Time

My suggestion to you is, it's time to turn the tables on the devil by making a decision. Today you're coming out of the pain of the past and going into a season of winning. Say this out loud now: "I am led by the Spirit of God. I have God's love on the inside of me. I am a lover and not a hater. Greater is He who lives in me than he who is in the world. In Christ, I am more than a conqueror over bitterness." Now get up and move toward the reality of this confession. Refuse to go back into bondage anymore.

Winning on the Inside

THE PATH TO CHANGE IS THROUGH
THE GLORY OF GOD.

Closing Remarks

Life is based on facts not fantasy. The facts are, you are someone special to God. That's a fact! Your life is valuable to Him. Winning is something you do every day when you decide to move forward—rather than backwards. Winning is something that you share with others. You never win by yourself, and you never win for yourself.

A victorious life comes from winning on the inside. Begin today to be what God made you to be. You are a winner!

"...they will recover."
Mark 16:18
"...fully restore them to strength."
(Fenton)
"...they will be restored to health."
(Wade)

Endnotes

[1] Added by author.

[2] Ibid.

[3] Ed Bulkley, Ph.D., "Why Christians Can't Trust Psychology" (Eugene, Oregon: Harvest House Publishers, 1993), pp. 107,117,118.

[4] Ibid.

[5] P. C. Nelson, "Bible Doctrines" (Gospel Publishing House, Springfield, Missouri, 1948), pp.12,13

[6] Ibid.

[7] A Cajun is a native of southern Louisiana. They are noted for their accent, love of life, and excellent cuisine. Even people living in Louisiana seem to disagree about the line of division between rednecks and Cajuns. When visiting Shreveport, Louisiana, I was told that anyone in Alexandria and below would be Cajun. After I moved to Alexandria, I learned that anyone south of Alexandria was really a Cajun.

[8] Merriam-Webster's Collegiate Dictionary, Tenth Ed., Springfield, MA: Merriam-Webster, Inc., 1996, pp. 20,381.

[9] Ibid., p. 266

[10] Kirbyjon H. Caldwell, *The Gospel of Good Success*, (Simon and Schuster, New York, New York, 1999), p. 212.

A Special Word
by Brian Bohrer

People who walk in bitterness live in an inward prison. Bitterness is the snakebite of the devil to destroy you and those around you, but God's Word is the snakebite kit! God's Word is your protection and the way to total freedom.

The Spirit of the Lord came unto me saying:

"It's time to step into freedom from bitterness. It's time to step into the freedom from the pain of the past that I have provided for you in My redemptive plan. Begin to celebrate your newfound liberty. My words spoken out of your mouth will break all the chains of bondage. Yes, I have given you My words. Use them carefully and they will produce freedom to you and to those to whom the Word is spoken. So get planted in My Word, stay in My Word, and refuse to speak anything else. Allow the Word to work in you, and the Word will take out the things that are holding you back and take you up to a higher level with your Father God.

"The victory that awaits you is already provided, it already belongs to those who will stand upon My Word. Victory is yours, now is the season for you to break forth and enter into the things that I have for you. Let it go, leave it behind, move on up and into a new way of living. For I have a plan for your life that must be fulfilled and will be fulfilled as you obey and release the things that hold you back. For there is coming an increase of My Spirit and an increase of My anointing that will only flow through those who have laid the necessary things aside. Don't allow the things that have happened to you keep you from entering into My great plan. As you enter into the plan that I have for your life, you will enter into a new door of anointing and a new door of miracles," says the Spirit of the Lord.

Will You Accept Jesus as Savior of Your Life Today?

The Bible says, "**That if thou shalt confess with thy mouth the Lord Jesus, and shalt believe in thine heart that God hath raised him from the dead, thou shalt be saved. For with the heart man believeth unto righteousness; and with the mouth confession is made unto salvation**" (Romans 10:9,10 KJV).

To receive Jesus Christ as Lord and Savior of your life, please pray this prayer from your heart today!

"Dear Jesus, I believe that You died for me and rose again on the third day. I believe with my heart that Jesus is the Son of God. I ask You to come into my life, forgive me of my sins, and give me eternal life. I confess You now as my Lord. Thank You for making me a new creation. Thank You for my salvation, in Your name I pray. Amen."

Confession for Freedom

Thank You for empowering me with Your Spirit, Lord, and for giving me a fresh hunger for Your Word.

As an act of my will, I forgive and release *(Name)* for the offenses he/she has inflicted upon me. I loose Your mercy and grace upon them, Lord, and I ask that You draw them by Your Spirit into Your family, in Jesus' name.

Thank You, Father, for freedom in You because of what Jesus did for me at Calvary. Today is the beginning of my celebration of liberation from bitterness. Today I walk in freedom. I am free in Jesus' name. Amen.

Winning on the Inside

FORGIVENESS IS ALWAYS THE
FIRST STEP TO RECOVERY.

Scripture References

All Scripture quotations marked KJV are taken from The King James Version of the Bible.

The Scripture quotations marked AMP are taken from *The Amplified Bible, Old Testament* copyright © 1964, 1987 by The Zondervan Corporation, Grand Rapids, Michigan. *The Amplified Bible, New Testament* copyright © 1958, 1987 by The Lockman Foundation, La Habra, California. Used by permission.

The Scripture quotation marked WEYMOUTH is taken from *The Weymouth Bible* by Richard Francis Weymouth. Copyright © 1909, The New Testament. James Clark and Company, London, England.

The Scripture quotations marked NIV are taken from *The New International Version* of the Bible. Copyright © 1973, 1978, 1984 by International Bible Society, Zondervan Publishing House, Grand Rapids, Michigan.

The Scripture quotation marked FENTON is taken from *The Holy Bible in Modern English* by Ferrar Fenton. Destiny Publisher, Massachusetts, n.d.

The Scripture quotation marked WADE is taken from *The New Testament Letters* by G. W. Wade. Copyright © 1934, Thomas Burby and Company, London, England.

The Scripture quotations marked JERUSALEM are taken from *The Jerusalem Bible.* Copyright © 1968, Doubleday and Company, Inc., New York, New York.

The Scripture quotations marked BASIC ENGLISH are taken from *The Bible in Basic English.* Copyright © 1965, University Press, Cambridge, England.

The Scripture quotation marked WUEST is taken from Kenneth S. Wuest, *The New Testament, An Expanded Translation.* Copyright © 1981, William B. Eerdmans Publishing Company, Grand Rapids, Michigan.

Special Message from the Author

I trust that you have found this book to be a blessing, and I pray that your walk with our Lord Jesus Christ will never be the same. If you would like to write us and give us your testimony on how this book has blessed you, it will be an encouragement to us.

If you need further material on salvation or the baptism in the Holy Spirit, we will be glad to send it to you free of charge.

For more information about Brian Bohrer Ministries and teaching materials, please write us.

Brian Bohrer

Brian Bohrer is the pastor of Living Bread Church in Washington, Missouri. He is a graduate of Rhema Bible Training Center and has been in full-time ministry for 28 years.

Pastor Brian was born again in a park in Bossier City, Louisiana, at the age of seven and was delivered from demonic influences at a Kathryn Kuhlman meeting in Tulsa, Oklahoma, in 1971.

Pastor Brian has appeared on Trinity Broadcasting Network with Jesse Duplantis and has his own radio broadcast, *Victorious Every Day* that is heard in the St. Louis area on KXEN, 1010AM Monday through Friday at 11:15 a.m.

Brian Bohrer is the author of several books including *Eye-Wired Men, ThinkOneCan, Winning on the Inside, Word Therapy, The Christian's Guide to Romance, Forgiveness, Discover Your Identity,* and *Wisdom and Money.*

Pastor Brian is ordained with RMAI and Mark Hankins Ministries.

To contact the author for meetings or speaking engagements, please use the information below:

Brian Bohrer Ministries

PO Box 1577 • Washington, MO 63090

Phone: (636) 239-5944

E-Mail: info@pastorbrian.org

Web Site: www.pastorbrian.org

Other Books by Brian Bohrer

Eye-Wired Men – *What every man needs to know about himself.*

Discover the keys to being the man that God designed you to be, a God-made man. This book reveals that men are faced with images of sex, lust, greed, and dealing with the power of wanting to be first and on top. This book has the real answers that you have been looking for, the secrets that keep a man in bondage, and the secrets that set a man free.

ThinkOneCan – *Take control of your life by taking control of your attitude.*

"Can't" is not in the Bible. "Can" is the language of the Bible. Your attitude is a gift from God to empower your life and to attract the right people into your life. You will discover the tools to empower your life and the gift to empower others.

Word Therapy – *Discover the creative power of your words.*

Applying God's Word by meditating and speaking His Word. Medical professionals are finding out that the thoughts of the mind and the words of the mouth are connected to many diseases in the body. God's Word tells us that positive thoughts and positive words have a healing effect upon the body. You can change your life by changing your words!

Making Peace with Your Past – *31 Days to Freedom.* This is a 31-day devotional that promotes freedom. Each page contains a declaration, an affirmation, and a powerful Scripture verse. As you meditate daily on the Word of God concerning forgiveness, you will begin to experience the peace of God that forgiveness brings.

Discover Your Identity – *The person you used to be is gone!*

You will gain access into the secrets of being a new creation, secrets that were "hidden from ages and generations," but that are now revealed to you IN CHRIST.

The Christian's Guide to Romance - *Discover 60 keys to empower your marriage.*

The teaching in this book will make a deposit in your marriage as Pastors Brian and Kimberly Bohrer share principles for marriage from God's Word and from their own experiences. As deposits are made into your marriage, you will be able to make withdrawals.

Wisdom & Money Workbook – *Motivating people to eliminate debts and create wealth through biblical solutions.* Being debt-free isn't just a dream! It can become a reality when you apply the simple, straightforward, step-by-step system taught in this workbook. Learn to become debt-free & loving it!

These books are available at: www.pastorbrian.org

CPSIA information can be obtained
at www.ICGtesting.com
Printed in the USA
FFHW02n1222230918
48547263-52435FF